The Standing Stones Speak

The Standing Stones Speak

Messages from the Archangels Revealed

Channeled by

NATASHA HOFFMAN
with
HAMILTON HILL

RENAISSANCE BOOKS
Los Angeles

From the Archangels to the human race

Library of Congress Cataloging-in-Publication Data
Archangels (Spirit)
        The standing stones speak / [channeled through] Natasha Hoffman and
    Hamilton Hill.
            p. cm.
        Includes index.
        ISBN 1-58063-191-6 (hardcover : alk. paper)
            I. Spirit writings. 2. Megalithic monuments—France—Carnac—Miscellanea.
    I. Hoffman, Natasha. II. Hill, Hamilton. III. Title.
    BF1301.A612 2001
    133.9'3—dc21   00-051831

10 9 8 7 6 5 4 3 2 1

Design by Jesús Arellano

All photos courtesy of Natasha Hoffman and Hamilton Hill unless otherwise noted.

Published by Renaissance Books
Distributed by St. Martin's Press
Manufactured in the United States of America
First edition

2/01
अम

Contents

Map

Preface

Our editor has asked me to say a little about ourselves and how we wrote this book. I have always been intuitive and able to see below the apparent surface of what happens on the physical plane, even in my earliest memories from childhood. I have also been aware that this ability in and of itself was not enough, that a psychic or clairvoyant aptitude does not reach high enough. One has to go to the highest Source, that of the creative energy of life itself, to the Creator. It is only the connection with the Creator that ultimately counts. Sadly, however, many people become seduced by the mere psychic level and go no further.

This understanding gave me the strength to bring up my four children—two girls and two boys—while working for twenty years as a college lecturer in art and design, with inspired guidance, in a small seaside town in England. Any difficulties I encountered I offered up to the Creator or the angels and always received immediate support—when I remembered to ask for it.

Knowing that my intuitive receiving could help people in a way that I felt teaching could not, I gave up being a lecturer, started to give personal readings, and practiced healing based on kinesiology. During this time I went through a period of personal transformation and life changes. After letting go of my roles as teacher and mother, when my children began to leave home I left as well, having outgrown the situation

I was in. I knew there was other work to be done but I had no idea what it might be. It was not until I stood among the stones at Carnac with my collaborator, Hamilton Hill, that I knew where the task lay and that this was the higher purpose of our being together. This was what our previous life experiences had prepared us for.

Hamilton has also come from an active, worldly life, for many years running a London business. Before that he studied history at Oxford University, then developed interests in archaeology and bee-keeping, and has spent much time sailing a boat in the English Channel. Leaving London, he became an organic farmer while his three children were growing up—a very fulfilling time for him—and later began working with the elements in another way as a designer of gardens. Each of these activities provided valuable years of experience in areas that although different are now interwoven. For Hamilton, farming and garden design led quite naturally to dowsing, and that in turn has made possible his input in the present work and his indispensable ability to give clarity to the message.

Dowsing is the ability to tap into cosmic consciousness, in which all knowledge is held and where all the answers can be found—we just have to learn what the questions are. It produces an inner "knowing," and can be effectively used by anyone after a little practice. For many years people around the world have been successfully locating underground water sources this way; some medical doctors have long used it for making diagnoses. Dowsing can also be a move toward the inner knowing that the early Gnostics had which goes beyond psychic ability.

If the inner quality of discernment is not developed, however, there will be no connection with the highest truth and it is foolish to act upon answers to questions that do not resonate with Love and an unselfish need for truth. When that is done, the response may then reflect personal wishes or can come from any discarnate and mischievous spirit of a lower level of being, which will take delight in interfering.

Dowsing is a bodily function, whether or not instruments such as a pendulum, metal L-rods, or other devices are used to assist the process. None of these tools moves of its own accord, but in response to the sensing of the body each can signal yes or no, positive or negative, or indicate a direction or location. It is not always necessary to use such a device as many people can dowse simply with their hands or their body and become trained "receptors" of information picked up from the immediate environment or from cosmic consciousness. We have used various dowsing methods to check the information contained in this book, but more often it was directly received in the mind.

I used a small pendulum—rose quartz, though the material is unimportant provided it suits you—to double-check my receiving and almost every word in the text, and ensure that the angels' message was adequately and correctly conveyed. Hamilton works better when using dowsing rods on site to access information about the actual energies around the stones, but he also used a pendulum when editing the text.

It was the Archangels' idea to include quotations at the beginning of each chapter. They got very excited about it, leading us to each book and the page where we would discover a relevant piece. They really

Stones at Kerzerho

wanted us to find human sayings that expressed something of what they wanted to convey.

The message contained in this book was received in various ways. Sometimes it came clearly as channeled writing. This, for me, was best, as when I stopped to work out what they were saying, I often got stuck and nothing happened. Sometimes I would get a visual answer to a question and then have to find the words. Sometimes there was a knowing without words, a real gnostic or mystical experience, and this was the hardest, because in my enthusiasm to explain, what I wrote down was often completely inadequate. I would pass it to Hamilton to edit, and he would read it and say, "It just doesn't make sense." I would look again and have to agree. This was very difficult for both of us as I knew what I needed to explain, and would shed tears of frustration at my own inadequacy to find the right words and at Hamilton's inability to intuit what I might mean without those words! But together we got it—it took a long time—and the process led to a greater clarity for us both about what was being expressed. There were many times when, experiencing problems, we'd rather have been sitting in a friendly French café eating croissants and sipping espresso instead of struggling to interpret the cosmic forces, but we were to find that treats were allowed us at opportune moments.

The quality of the information received, especially when dowsing, depends not only upon the recipient's sensitivity, but also on the integrity and ability to distinguish between what is the truth, what is part of the truth—and what is a deliberate red herring. Right at the start, for example, we found ourselves receiving garbled and confusing information from what turned out to be decoy stones (more on that later). An attitude of respect is needed.

We became aware that the messages which follow came from beings we may call the Archangels, partly through the very high level of energy that surrounded us when we worked with them, and also because they didn't say immediately who they were, but waited for us to ask, which in due time we did. Throughout the process, we had other, more direct, experiences of their very powerful presence. On one occasion, right after we had started our work, I woke to find a very tall being beside me. All I could see was the tall shape, but I sensed a feeling of concern. It was not an Archangel, nor one of our spirit friends, who all have different ways of identifying themselves and certain colors around them. It spoke in a surprisingly loud, masculine voice: "You will have to give up all your old ways of thinking and you must tell 'him' this, too." I knew it was an angel. It spoke so loudly that I was sure Hamilton heard it as well, but no, he was still asleep. On another occasion I was told, "You are not just writing this down for others, you know, you have to live it, you are part of this and you cannot separate yourselves from it. You yourselves must become the Rainbow Warriors, or you cannot help others so to become."

This event led us to include some of what we experienced along our journey that helped us to attune to the Archangels' messages. Several little personal episodes appear in between a number of the chapters that follow.

As we were nearing the end of the messages, the Archangels told me, "It often seems that people believe life is a competition for suffering, and humans think of so many ways of undergoing and inflicting it. You are addicted to suffering," they went on, "because you have been made to feel guilty about joy, and this is a dangerous situation which so dulls the senses to happiness that only the suffering has value for you."

Occasionally, when the information was coming through clearly and directly, my mind would race ahead and I wanted to add bits from my own thoughts. Then I would be told very firmly (there was always an angel looking over my shoulder as I wrote), "Yes, that's very interesting but it's not what we are saying, so take it out." Sometimes it was the reverse. I wanted to take bits out I wasn't happy with and would remove part of the text, yet I couldn't get it out of my mind. Then I would be told, "You have to include this, put it back!"

A specific example of this is included in the final chapter, about possible future events, in particular the threat to Earth from a meteorite. Remember, a prediction is something which is predestined and cannot be changed, while a prophecy is something which certain eventualities are likely to bring about, but might not happen if the actual events leading up to it can be altered and no longer call it into being.

One of my daughters related to me a dream she had when she was ten years old, in which she saw a meteorite bound for Earth. She knew it did not have to make impact, seeing people all over the planet holding hands in peace and love; but she also saw people who didn't believe it was possible to change events and went out to have a last wild party.

Within this latter group of people she was aware that there was much abuse and pollution of mind and body, as opposed to the honoring and true celebration of life. It was truly a battle between the higher and lower forces of humanity. My daughter knew with certainty that if all these people held hands and united in loving strength, in an honoring of each other and the Creator, then the meteorite would not hit the Earth. There was no conclusion to the dream—just two possible endings and a choice to be made. On hearing this, I knew that I could not omit that uneasy but important part of the message.

We hope you enjoy reading this book and, like us, feel inspired by what the Archangels have given to us all.

—*Natasha Hoffman*

Introduction

One moonlit evening in Carnac we thought to visit the stones by night. At Le Ménec Alignment the wicket gate was unlocked, so we slipped into the enclosure and stood quietly inside for a moment. In the sky pale clouds drifted across a full Moon. As we moved into the avenues of stone we were surprised to find a small black cat walking with us. A few minutes later a man also entered and, not seeing us in the dark, gently placed his hand on top of a stone for some moments as though taking a temperature reading. The cat stayed at our feet and all three of us watched silently as the man strode over to the specially imposing monolith in the fourth row; this is the stone from which most of the information in this book has been gleaned. After lingering there he turned, walked along the outer row, and left by the gate. What was he doing? Greeting old friends? Perhaps he wanted to check the emanations, but the Sun's rays had gone and the pulsation of incoming light energy cannot be felt at night. Certainly he was one of the many people on the planet who are becoming aware that these ancient megaliths have preserved things of importance to our lives today.

We too walked over to the menhir with the friendly little cat, who seemed very much at home in the somewhat eerie landscape of standing stones silhouetted against a moonlit sky. Earlier that day we had reactivated a sacred site where the energy flow had long ceased, and we now felt that the cat had been sent as a messenger to confirm that all was well there. It played happily around our feet until we left. No doubt its perceptions were keener than ours.

The enormous stone with its curious shape, known as *Le Géant*—the Giant—marks the intersection of three "leylines," or straight bands of solar energy. The principal leyline is a wide, easily dowsable band of energy running north-south as a line of longitude. Our dowsing indicates that it passes through Wales and England, connecting with the Castlerigg stone circle in Northumbria, across Scotland and then, encircling the globe, goes on to link the two Poles. At Carnac it is almost 800 yards in width, taking in much of the principal Le Ménec Alignment. There are many other solar bands in the area, on which every monument is carefully placed. Perhaps the giant menhir, the original stone on the site, was not surprisingly chosen by the Archangels to embody a message.

"It's a library," Natasha said in surprise one day, looking at the rows of stones all around, "and we can read it." That is how this book was started. It consists of channeled readings from five of the huge number of standing stones in the Morbihan district of Brittany on the Atlantic coast of France. Who encoded the information? And why? We are told that it was put there and has been continuously updated by the Archangels, who have the responsibility for the evolution of our planet, so that it becomes available at a time when such guidance can help humanity to move forward. We understand that there are other places in the world where more information has been encoded. There are decoy systems, too, which prevent access by those with intent to distort or misuse it for their own ends. We had to gain the trust of the stones, proving our friendship, before they would tell us which of their number held the messages. These messages are not defined by language or time, and can be read by direct receiving or by question-and-answer dowsing. They emerge as contemporary, up-to-date information and guidance for the new age of Aquarius, for the experience of living in the truth and understanding the relevance of the teachings of the masters from all ages.

The country around Carnac has one of the largest assemblies of megalithic remains on the planet. It is a much-visited World Heritage Site. There are great chambered mounds—one, Kercado, dated to about 6,700 years ago—many dolmens, stone enclosures and single menhirs, and the famous alignments of standing stones (see the glossary at the back of this book) dating from before 3000 B.C. The stones were set up by groups of seafaring folk who settled there, people of peaceful habits and considerable skills. They had a knowledge of astronomy from long observations of the sky in what was then a time of settled weather, and they knew well the cycles of the Sun and Moon. Inspired by a source of higher intelligence, they were able to build and orient large structures of stone for ritual purposes, aligned to lunar and especially solar events such as sunrise or sunset at midwinter or midsummer. Kercado, for example, is placed so that the Sun penetrates its inner chamber at the moment of midwinter sunrise—a sign of rebirth and the continuity of life.

These impressive megalithic remains of the late Stone Age are scattered around western Europe from Malta to Scandinavia, and are especially numerous along the Atlantic seaboard, on the hills and near the rivers in Spain, Portugal, France, and the British Isles. Over a span of some three thousand years, until the introduction and general use of metal, they were important as local ceremonial centers and as markers of the energy networks which wrap around our globe. They have given rise to stories that they were put there by so-called supernatural beings, that they belong to the "faery kingdom," and so on—all, of course, considered hostile in the eyes of the Church, if not "works of the devil"! Often the subconscious mind is aware of presences at such antique places and, without some deeper awareness or an open mind, a confused picture can emerge. Actually there is an element of truth in all the stories, for they are home to other, invisible, beings who play a role at these sacred places alongside the animals, the plants, and us. We hope their existence and functions emerge with more clarity as you read on.

Incidentally, do not think of the Druid priests in this connection; they entered western Europe much later, with the Celtic incomers, not long before Julius Caesar conquered them in Gaul and made the first Roman landing in Britain. Their ritual places were in woodland clearings, in the sacred groves of oak and ash, not at Stonehenge, where modern Druidry likes to assemble.

At Carnac, as elsewhere, the great stone and earthen mounds held the bones of the first important ancestors. The dolmens are ritual chambers, once covered by a cairn of stones, repositories of the bones of the members of each local tribe or family group, venerated for many years and replaced from time to time by others of the community dead. None was simply a place of burial, but a combination of temple and tomb. They were used over generations for ceremonies involving libations and dedicatory bone-fires. Above all, in each season of the farming year people recognized and honored the power of the Sun, which makes life possible.

The cromlechs, or gathering places—rounded enclosures of close-packed stones—were laid out for larger communal assemblies and ceremonies to mark such important events as the regular rebirth of the Sun, joyful and festive seasonal occasions that drew together people from the surrounding clans and others from more distant places.

Beautifully polished stone artifacts, talismans for exchange and ritual, have been found. Elaborately incised stone slabs are hidden within some of the early ossuary chambers, like those at Newgrange in Ireland and on the island of Gavrinis in Brittany. Their swirling curves and spiral patterns hold a dowsable field of energy, alternately positive and negative, which both embodies and symbolizes the energy needed for regeneration, for rebirth after death, for the journey of the soul back to its heavenly origin. Clearly the megalithic people were aware of the life force reaching them on the rays of the Sun and sustaining fertility day after day, year after year. Provided due honor was paid to the unseen forces, these people could continue to live in harmony with nature and one another in a long continuity of custom, focused in each territory on the sacred stones they had set up.

The long avenues of the principal alignments at Carnac extend over some two and a half miles and contain nearly three thousand stones of varying size and shape; there were many more before the stone-robbing and destruction of recent centuries. The alignment at Kerzerho near Erdeven to the west still has more than a thousand massive pieces of granite, although the cromlech enclosure has virtually disappeared. At Le Ménec and elsewhere the original processional approach has been gradually extended with the addition of other lines of stones over countless generations of use.

The significant placing of the single stones and every sacred structure upon the energetic solar network of leylines which crisscrosses the landscape here occurs all over the globe, from the temples of Egypt, India, and Central and South America, to the innumerable sacred places of Europe and Asia. When the man-made monuments of antiquity were located on such sites, it was with full awareness of their solar vitality and fundamental importance for Earth and all its variety of living forms.

Until recent centuries, Chinese geomancers, Native Americans, adherents to the Muslim faith, and the Christian Church have continued this perception of sacred places within a global energy network, siting their shrines and ceremonial buildings according to the example of their neolithic forebears. We illustrate this in relation to the stones and the churches of Carnac in the map on the following pages; roads, which are mostly straight and would confuse the picture, are not shown.

The fine menhir of Le Manio near Kermario, twenty feet in height, yielded the general information that forms the second chapter. The remaining chapters come from four individual stones, two at Le Ménec, two at Kerzerho, which are programmed with the more specific information and guidance that we have been able to draw upon; but all of them contain a powerful, slow-moving life force and a form of memory. This is made possible by the crystalline structure of granite, which, as with the ubiquitous crystal microchips in computers, has the piezo-electric potential to produce an electric current under heat or pressure. Conversely, applied electric power produces a constant resonance and enables information to be stored and time to be kept. Retrieval in this case is a function of the mind, the brain itself being electronically and chemically powered to suit the human intention. You may ask, as we did, why it was necessary to encode the standing stones with information rather than put it directly into the human mind. We were told that stone anchors the message to the Earth in a way that a person, who is not only mobile but short-lived, cannot. Granite is ancient consciousness, something rooted in the Earth that "has been here since life began."

It is the purpose of this book to share the messages we have received, so that the wounds of the human heart caused by past misinterpretation of the truths of creation may be healed, and the intuitive mind may be reawakened to the real function of human life: the opening of the heart to the harmonies of the cosmos.

—*Natasha Hoffman and Hamilton Hill*

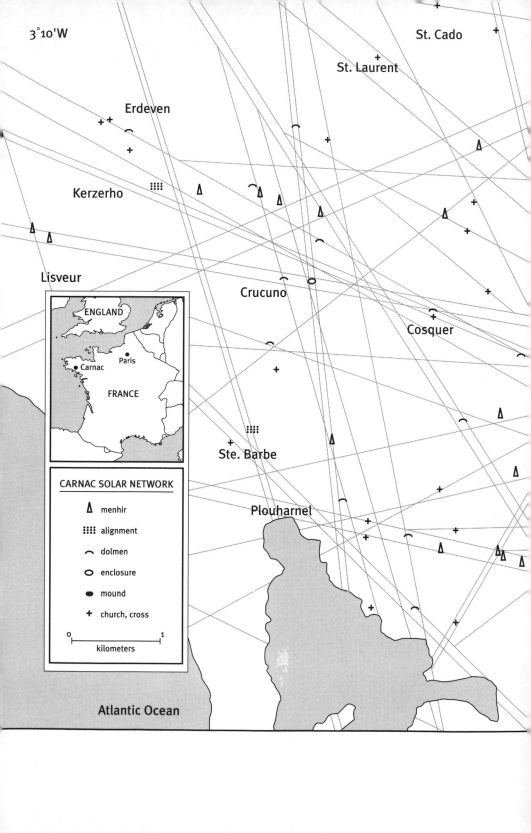

3°10'W

St. Cado

St. Laurent

Erdeven

Kerzerho

Lisveur

ENGLAND

Paris
Carnac

FRANCE

Crucuno

Cosquer

CARNAC SOLAR NETWORK

Λ   menhir

⁞⁞⁞⁞ alignment

⌒   dolmen

○   enclosure

●   mound

+   church, cross

0   1
kilometers

Ste. Barbe

Plouharnel

Atlantic Ocean

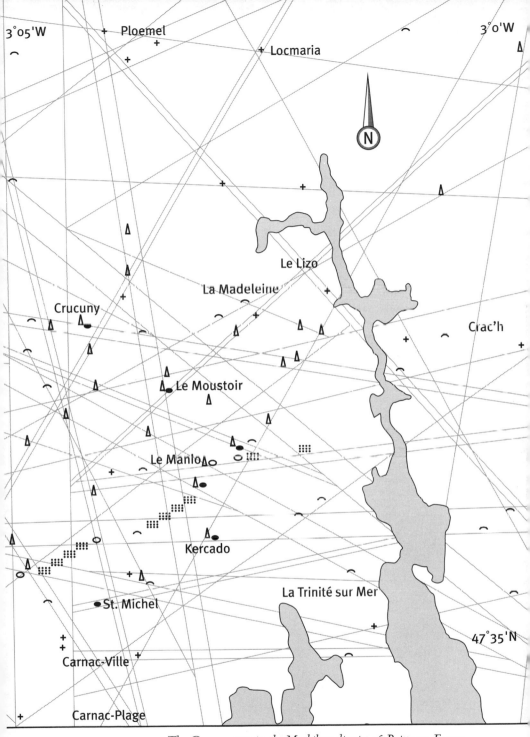

The Carnac area in the Morbihan district of Brittany, France

Of the many things which mankind has forgotten,

your origins,

the presence of the Archangels,

and the purpose of the standing stones

are three of the most important.

Le Géant at Le Ménec

CHAPTER 1

The Megaliths

We see the disintegrating process that is going on in the world. The social order is breaking down, the various religious organizations, the beliefs, the moral and ethical structures . . . are all failing. Throughout our so-called civilization . . . there is corruption and every form of useless activity.

—Krishnamurti

The message we want to give you, which you are reading in the context of your own time and place, was first encoded in the standing stones at Carnac by those of us whom you call the Archangels. It is a continuous process, which we began soon after the end of the First World War. It was that global conflict which marked the start of the current process of disintegration; it was then that your lack of understanding of cosmic law or concern for global harmony began to disturb the balance, not just of the planet Earth but of the universe itself. It was truly a watershed in the history of your world, a moment when we felt it necessary to intervene. Now, your society's divorce from the spirit is a process which is bringing about the decline of the human race, and this has become more evident with the domination of destructive technology and materialism in almost every part of the world.

The ancient standing stones upon your planet were set up by your ancestors as a fail-safe device for attracting into the fabric of Earth the vital energies of life, which are transmitted on the rays of the Sun and in other cosmic forces. In a similar manner, your chakra system continually receives an input of energy for maintaining the life force in the body and its organs. In each case, then, there are specific locations, entry points, for that essential inflow of the solar force. You have various names for those special energy points on the surface of the Earth; we call them the sacred places because they are dedicated to the Creator's purposes.

The megaliths are activators and visual reminders of the cosmic forces. They act a little like acupuncture needles in the Earth's surface, maintaining and stimulating the flow of vital energy where it is needed. Their stones, uncontaminated by the Fall, hold a power of Love equal to that of the angels, which vibrates directly with the human heart chakra. They are transformers which facilitate regeneration; without them, the energies would not be sufficiently focused. The intention of those who set them up was to enhance the light of the Creator by providing sanctuaries for themselves where an essential resonance with the cosmos could be celebrated. So the principal megaliths mark the receiving points where the nutrition of the subtle energies, needed for the perpetual renewal of each season's cycle of growth, was perceived to enter Earth, and others, the dolmens and the menhirs, were sited on the energy bands which link those points. Accordingly, every important work of construction, whether earthen mound or henge, timber shrine or stone temple, was carefully located in the landscape for its protection from disharmony, upon an energy line or a sacred site.

These energetic places upon the Earth, of which the megaliths are the sentinels, had already been set out by us at an earlier time, beginning before the fall of Atlantis. Our input created a blueprint of divine intention for the balancing of energies within and upon the Earth; it ensures that if this balance is too far disturbed, the Earth has the power within itself to right the situation or to attract cosmic forces to do so. If the Creator's blueprint is not adhered to by human beings the planet will, in due time, act to restore order. At this moment you are at that delicate, in-between point, when we see that there is still time to prevent great devastation. There is time to choose to correct the imbalance, for you to achieve a conscious cosmic harmony.

The placement of the great stones and shrines of various kinds was overminded by our presence and inspired by certain memories in human minds from the time of Atlantis. The actual construction was carried out by local groups of people, extended families of men and women, during your Neolithic period. At that time there was still a form of conscious communication between humans and the angelic realm which lightened the task of raising the stones; we were able to give instruction in the use of certain frequencies of sound, which by chanting and concerted action reduce the effect of gravity.

The structures built in this way became places, protected and powerful, for regular gatherings of each community, for the holding of ceremonies which venerated life as well as death as rites of passage. Earthly and cosmic cycles were recognized and celebrated there as periodic events in each year. Some still have a tenuous survival in the later religious structures at those same places.

This was a time when travel by beings from other celestial spheres was openly acknowledged. There was much coming and going from some of these megalithic sites, a few of which were—and still are— used as cosmic airports, although without the need for any physical vehicle. Earth beings, too, who know the initiatory process can make use of these portals to journey out of body to the planets or even other galaxies. We set the portals in place; the stones to mark and anchor them were erected by humankind later—as, for example, within the western cromlech of Le Ménec at Carnac.

Those who traveled through these gateways to other dimensions of being brought back with them knowledge to sustain and advance the Earth and its inhabitants, all of whom are dependent for physical life upon solar and other cosmic energies. Gradually, however, over the centuries, this link with other worlds diminished until eventually we came to see that men and women were no longer living in accordance with the divine plan, that they had lost the understanding of their place in the cosmic order. We saw that humans had forgotten their origins. Their evolution and that of the planet was not going according to plan, and it became clear that the seeds of future disintegration had been planted. It was decided then to program certain stones at Carnac, and a few elsewhere, with the truth about the origins of humankind and, more significantly, with a message of encouragement to enable a balance to be restored.

Our aim is to help you to create a new way of life on the Earth and so return to the wider harmony of the universe itself.

When we first began to establish the sacred places of power, we realized that the Fall from Grace had already permeated human consciousness, but we could not know how far that Fall would be. We intended humanity to redress the imbalance by remaining connected to the Divinity within themselves, but darkness has enveloped the human mind. Now, despite peacemaking treaties, international talks, and sporadic goodwill activities, human participation in keeping your home, the Earth, alive and healthy has been ineffectual and has almost ceased. Any communication with the divine Source of life is regarded as an option. Indeed, most human activity has become destructive as it has lost that connection to motivate it. The universe is starting to suffer because pollution in the human mind has led to the physical worldwide pollution of the planet, insidious in its far-reaching effects on other planets and beyond.

Our purpose is to remind you that, as human beings, you have a special function as transformers of cosmic energy, the same task that has long been carried out at the sacred sites and symbolized for you by the megaliths and structures of former generations. You have a responsibility to raise your level of vibration, both spiritually and physically, and in so doing, raise that of your planet. Working with the natural order and within your physical limitations will achieve this; going against the flow of nature and its rhythms will not.

In turn, your planet acts as a transformer of the energies which flow into it through the focal points of the sacred sites. Obstructing or neglecting this daily natural flow creates blockages in the process of human and planetary evolution. False materialistic goals posing as progress, and a lack of awareness of the vital significance of the cosmic energy patterns, have impeded your development and your attunement with soul. There is an intensity of disharmony caused, for example, by the increasing pollution of water, excessive traffic in the air and on highways, buildings in unsuitable areas, the widespread use of laboratory-made chemicals, and the expanding fields of electromagnetic interference in the atmosphere. All of these counteract the natural balance by superimposing negative flows of man-made energy upon the positive original structure.

If the light of true spiritual understanding were brought into the human mind and body it would shine out, and matter would respond by harmoniously serving humanity. Without that light-inspired essence of spirituality, matter becomes dark and heavy and exerts an excessive, controlling power over humanity. An acquisitive society cannot re-create harmony on the planet.

You will soon be experiencing a stronger input of cosmic energies—some of you are already—which will influence the Earth and raise your personal awareness through your chakras, in preparation for a new enlightenment in the times to come. They will be opening you where, until now, you have been closed in heart and mind. In the past, souls of great light have been sent to help you through periods of darkness by awakening you to spirit. In this present time, we, the Archangels, are acting as the necessary mediators between physical life and the divine.

If our message touches your heart, remember the bearers of it, the standing stones; there is an empathy between stone and angel. Although stone, like you, is a part of evolution, while angels are not, both are vital elements in the re-creation of balance and harmony on Earth.

The purpose of life is evolution of the soul, not of the species, and evolution depends on the ability of the personality to learn from any given situation. There are no direct paths to truth or enlightenment, only ways of changing your consciousness to perceive earthly reality as a part of the whole.

Your planet has passed through a dark period of history, a time when it did not matter whether the learning process seemed positive or negative, except that the unconscious choice affected the quality of your daily lives. What did matter was whether the learning was effective. In the times to come it will be of the utmost importance that learning is through positive, life-enhancing choices. Only they can release you from the patterns of fear that so restrict evolution of the soul.

Many people will find themselves in situations which enable them to confront old karmic patterns. Until repetitive patterns are broken, the resulting unresolved karmic links will continue to check the soul's evolution. If the change cannot be made in the present incarnation, it will have to happen in spirit, that is, after bodily death, which is more difficult because help on several levels is required. There will be no opportunity for these souls to return to Earth as before, continuing to replay their particular dramas on the planet; they will be resolved in another dimension.

After a certain period of time, new conditions on the globe and in the heavens will no longer allow the reenactment of those old negative patterns. Any pockets of negativity which persist, wherever they collect, will all be blown away like dust, and only stone and angel will remain to guide those who are left. That is why we have had to intervene.

An Adventure in Time

This little adventure started at the beginning of time. All of us were there: the Archangels; you, the reader; and we, the present scribes.

We, in our inner knowing, became aware of a task to be done but did not yet know what it was to be. We had a notion that it would combine our different abilities in some constructive way.

During a healing session many years ago, before I had even heard of Carnac, I was told of a place in France where there were many standing stones and that it was important that I go there. I felt this was interesting and then clean forgot about it. A few years later, while visiting my cousin and his family, who live on the edge of Dartmoor, the wildest part of Devon, I noticed on the tea table a biscuit tin, sent to them by friends. There upon its lid was a painting of the Carnac alignments, the endless rows of ancient standing stones. It felt like an electric shock: this was where I had to go, I knew it instantly, as the picture glowed quietly on the table. I had finally gotten the message.

Sometime later Hamilton and I found ourselves at Carnac. I had the feeling that we were visiting very special relations, old friends. There was a timeless quality and vast strength around those stones, and it was so comfortable to be in their presence. We felt very welcome.

At that time there was no fence around the main alignments and we could wander freely, soaking up the atmosphere, sometimes touching the stones. Occasionally we bumped into other people around one menhir or another, people who were also completely absorbed by the place, and this led to some interesting exchanges, especially when we started dowsing with rods and a pendulum.

The timing of that visit was perfect, as on later occasions a steel barrier had been put up to protect the monuments from soil erosion and being clambered on by children—although I had a feeling that the stones enjoyed this interaction with the young people's vitality. Now the site is undergoing restoration in an attempt to save it from further damage, but eventually some access will again be allowed. It is interesting to note that our encounters with other people and our conversations about life and esoteric "energies," which came so easily amidst the stones, did not take place later when one could only stand and look at them through the fencing.

It was then, within a few minutes of arriving at the site that first time, as we were walking between the lines, that I heard the voice in my head, saying "this is a library," and realized that I was able to read it. I was close to that very large stone in the main avenue, the Giant, and the voice seemed to come from that odd-looking monolith. Even then I was not altogether unfamiliar with the idea that stones are alive, have memory, and so can be record keepers.

As there are so many standing stones in Carnac, we had to find the right one to start with. By using a map and dowsing over the model in the excellent archaeological museum in Carnac Town, we were led to another great menhir, isolated somewhere in the woods at a place called Le Tertre du Manio.

A rough track led us past a riding school with ponies and some hardy children riders. It was raining by this time, and Le Manio seemed to be lost in the trees. It was not well signposted and we took several wrong turns in the wood, sometimes losing each other as we took different routes. I was in favor of coming back when the Sun was out, when suddenly we came upon it in a small clearing. It is an imposing menhir, the tallest in the area, and appears to be leaning slightly in an attempt to reach down and communicate with the humans below. Its slender elegance is set off by the surrounding pine trees. Near it is a four-sided arrangement of smaller stones. No one else was there, so we sat on a fallen tree and "tuned in." Feeling slightly in awe of the strong presence, I made some notes. After about an hour it began to rain more heavily and a group of people arrived, so we took our leave. We had been given information that surprised us, that the standing stones within the alignments have been programmed with a message for the human race. We learned that it had been put there by an angelic presence, to be found at the right time, and that it would help us all to reconnect with our roots in the past so that we, the human race, can go forward into the future with new respect for our own sacred planet.

Dining at our hotel later that evening, and still slightly in shock at our experience, we found that two English people at the next table were a couple we had spoken to, trying out our poor French, in the alignments. They too were on a quest.

The next day, inspired by Le Tertre du Manio, we forgot to proceed with caution and due respect, and went back into the stone rows. Silence. Not a murmur. I tried a group of three stones, huddled together, but what I "received" from them was so depressing and without hope that it was like being called into the headmaster's office for a reprimand. We spent time working on this information but finally had to accept that it was not at all the encouraging message we had been led to expect. What to do? Had we encroached upon the stones, the mineral domain, without permission? From time to time we have been helped by conversations with White Bull, a spirit guide, a Native American in his most recent incarnation, who has given indications and left us to do the work. So now we went to him to ask what was going on.

"There are decoys," he told us, "you must go back and make friends with the stones of Carnac before you can find the three or four which hold and will reveal the information you want; one of them will guide you to the others." On our return we spoke silently to the guardians of place, announcing our presence, and asked permission to be shown the stones with the message. There was an almost audible chatter and we found, quite simply, that the first stone was our old friend, the Giant in Le Ménec Alignment. So much information came to us then, and in such confusing detail, that we almost forgot there were other stones. They introduced themselves later, and the messages began to take shape. That is how this story came to be written for you.

—*Natasha*

CHAPTER 2

Harmony

Love all and hate none,
Mere talk of peace will avail you naught.
Mere talk of God and religion will not take you far.
Bring out all of the latent powers of your being
And reveal the full magnificence
Of your immortal self.
Be surcharged with peace and joy
And scatter them wherever you go.

— Hazrat Khwaja Mu'inuddin Chishti, Sufi saint

The words of this message are for now; they are a call to heart, a call to spirit, a call to soul.

Love exists as a powerful force in the universe and especially upon the Earth. Sometimes it is felt as a terrible force. Love can be devastating when it teaches you the lessons of life, showing you what is not Love, releasing you from illusions, opening your eyes. It can be as gentle as a breeze upon your arm when you listen, or as destructive as a volcanic eruption when you do not.

There will always be divine Love. It is a universal creative force. When it exists as a guiding force in your life on Earth you will become true to your real self. Through this message you will see who that real self is and come to know the greater whole of which you are a part.

Menhir at Le Tertre du Manio

Negativity upon the planet cannot be transformed without the dynamic power of the Creator's Love. The only thing that grows in the absence of Love is bitterness.

When, long ago, we arranged for the networks of planetary energy to be set up around the Earth, our intention was that they would resonate with the Source of all life, and so allow the development and expression of a lifestyle for humanity in complete concord with cosmic principles and natural rhythms. Earth is an integral part of the cosmos, moving in harmony within the solar system. If it is out of balance with itself, this affects not only the solar system but the whole universe. By projecting the energy patterns of the cosmos onto your planet Earth, we intended to provide you with a global life-support system which would reflect all the rhythmic energies of the universe in an inner and all-pervasive flow of energetic qualities, which in turn is repeated in the human body through the blood and physical organs.

There is a sympathetic resonance between the human body and the body of the Earth; they are made of the same stuff. If people are not harmonious, then neither is the planet, and for us this lack of harmony can be felt in the cosmos too; you are no longer at one with the Creator. The truth of creation has become obscured; your inner life no longer reflects the outer harmony of creation. Human beings once were in balance with their environment and attuned to the life force. The harmonious flow of that force was reflected in a cyclical, rhythmic way of living, with awareness of the regular movements of the heavenly bodies. Ceremonies were held throughout the year to mark the successive seasons governed by the Sun, the necessary periodic times of dormancy, planting, and harvesting. There was an understanding of the existence and functions of unseen celestial beings in the observance of those natural cycles, and of the importance for the Earth of the energy networks that we had put into place upon it.

The ability to respond to and work with those rhythmic patterns has to be restored in humankind. Reconnecting with your own inner light, finding the means to listen and understand the truth within you, will lead you back to working with the light of the universe. It is the power of intuition which can restore in you that understanding which earlier inhabitants of planet Earth were able to share, when the light of the Sun was reflected in the human aura.

The wisdom that will enable you to link with the divinity of cosmic forces has been held in safekeeping for you. It is your inheritance. Now that there is such a growing need for greater conscious awareness, it is time to integrate once more with the celestial wisdom that surrounds the planet. New energy from your celestial guardians and your cosmic families is available for this, to help in finding your true direction by bringing balance back into human life.

At one time, the emotions were a simple spontaneous response to each natural occurrence. They had not become projections of anxiety and fear as they are now. Emotions have evolved down a negative route and become full of shadows, untrustworthy guides. For humanity to raise its vibrations and regain lost dignity, each of you has to learn to work with a higher level of sensitivity, bringing love to the forefront and making use of the right-brain wisdom which comes from intuitive knowing.

This negativity of the lower emotions, which is fed by fear and breeds hatred among you, has clouded and distorted the truth. The aura of the Earth is now clogged with the grief of the many souls who have experienced life after life in which the distortion of spiritual truths and the loss of true human feelings have separated them from the light and Love of the Creator.

For thousands of years you have lived without honoring natural laws. You have replaced spiritual law with man-made laws that are based on power and control; they are unrelated to the natural harmonies of the universe.

Only the light of the Creator can penetrate these shadows and change the vibrations of Earth. As many of you start to heal your own pain, you can draw that light into your bodies, opening up to change. All of you have absorbed too much pain and suffering in successive lives; you have too little "dance energy" in you, compared to those early people who used dance and song as a sacred link between heaven and earth, as a means of achieving balance in their lives. By dance and celebration they honored the seasons in ways which revitalized the flow of divine energy within and without. Both planet and people need spiritual nourishment, which comes through the Love that blesses and honors the cycles and all the changes within life. Honoring the flow eases the pain of letting go, releasing that which you cling to in fear, and allows you to move forward within the pattern of eternal change, finding your own due place within it.

The prolonged period of separation from any conscious interaction with cosmic rhythms has caused many of you to find little meaning in your daily lives. You have created a superficial order in an effort to replace the natural order of things, and now it is collapsing in upon itself because it is unsupported by the universe. To live in harmony, it is essential to establish an inner as well as an outer connection with the divine. You can do this by tuning in to that sacred space inside each of you, where everything is still. It is there that answers can be found, by listening to the inner teacher—your higher self—distinguishing it from the lower self, which speaks through negative emotions. As the sage Lao-tzu said, "I know the way of all things by what is inside me." The inner purpose for incarnated humanity is to awaken to that soul force within, recreating the unity and balance that can merge all shadows into the light.

When a society or civilization only acknowledges one aspect of itself, such as those people whose beauty seems fashionable or desirable, or those who have wealth, popular talents, or charisma, it is rejecting those who appear to have nothing to offer: the beggars and those who are difficult to love. What becomes manifest, then, is the pain of lack of love; it becomes a negative force to be reckoned with. If the negativity is accepted, embraced, it has the power to enrich the community; but ignored it will draw in the shadows and accentuate the social divisions with violent actions that come from bitterness of heart. You have seen this in your media so many times and in so many places. It is vital, therefore, that every human being shall feel the restorative power of light and Love. If the human heart and mind are tuned to the frequency of Love, the planet can be restored to health and made whole again. If your society cannot learn to do this, the planet will renew itself without your consent, and many of you will be removed in the process.

For too long you have been separated from what is essential to human life, that is, the experience of the Creator's Love. We are intervening at this time in your history to open your hearts to that Love which we can bring to you, if you are willing to receive it.

Realize that the energy field of our angelic realm is very powerful. Human beings who have failed to develop the true strength of sensitivity would be overwhelmed and fearful in our presence; only when you are familiar with the power of Love can you stand in the presence of angels without fear. If you lose your fear and can raise your vibrations through Love, we can meet you, and extend our Love to reach your level of being.

You are never alone, although many of you feel lonely and unconnected. We have always been with you, but because Earth's vibrations until recently have been so dense, we have been unable to enter your lives and touch you; with the exception of some of those whom you have called saints, whose personal vibrations had a certain purity that allowed them to have a direct experience of divine energy. They have served to remind others that it is possible to reach it, that it is ever present. In times to come, many more of you will be able to experience the presence of those beings of higher frequency who can illuminate your way.

More of you are now looking for that inner peace and personal fulfillment by turning to spiritual or creative practices. As you do so with sincerity, and without abandoning your daily work, you will start to experience a state of inner joy which is far removed from the attitudes and systems of belief which have for so long controlled both mind and body. Finding that joy will provide a sanctuary from the judgmental system of reward and punishment that has dominated every civilization, reducing your sensitivity and separating you from the divine essence.

At this time, the human race has an opportunity to make progress by understanding how the condition of Earth has an effect on the solar system and how the other planets affect Earth, their combined energies working together to maintain the physical balance and supply the spiritual qualities of life. As you start to appreciate this essential interaction, you will be recharged with the desire to evolve and supported in this by the angels and our other celestial helpers.

All forms of life have an electromagnetic identity, a measurable field of vibratory energy. This includes the life forms you cannot see, your angelic helpers. We and you give out and receive signals continuously on different frequencies, like a radio with many stations. The energy wavelengths of your own thoughts can inhibit you or free you. The power of thought is the power of creation, since matter follows thought. Thought creates the quality of your life. It affects your emotions which, whether they are suppressed or flowing freely, affect your bodily health and your environment. Know that your thoughts are not private; they can be heard by us and sensed by the higher selves of others. Thoughts bring into being all manner of diverse energies that affect you and others and actually construct the pattern of your life.

Earth has many places of power where the standing stones still remain, and there people can go to feel reenergized, there you may make contact with the cosmic healing forces. Within a stone circle, you can be shielded from the disturbing effects of the tangle of crossed wires, the electromagnetic fields and thoughts that fill the air, night and day, cluttering the atmosphere and making it difficult to think straight. Changing your own energy field at such a place makes it possible to cut through this frenetic barrier. Raising your own vibrations at a sacred site will enhance the energy of the place as well as your own. Each such place is a natural focus for the etheric energies of the Earth and of the cosmos, so as to combine their power. This is symbolized by the spire of a church or the minaret of a mosque. Each is built on a site of power with a view to drawing down the cosmic forces to revitalize the Earth, a process which can be reactivated and utilized by the power of human intention.

Now, as in the past, the root of the problems in human life is the lack of spiritual intention or awareness behind your ceaseless activities. Your institutions and establishments have no such input; it is rarely found in the occasional human enterprise that is inspired and truly blessed. Knowledge of the spiritual forces needs to be reawakened, together with the ability to integrate it into every aspect of human life.

Until now the human race has been unable to "receive" clearly and harmoniously because the left and right parts of the brain have been out of balance with each other. The logical, calculating, left hemisphere has dominated the intuitive, direct-sensing right, so that most human action has not been inspired but calculated with the intellect, and therefore limited as the intellect is limited. Similarly, the lack of balance between male and female energy has caused great difficulties for you all. It is time to learn how to balance the functions of the various parts of the brain and the different qualities of women and men, so that you may work together in harmony with the other beings of the universe.

We see that technology is continuing to advance without any spiritual motivation. What you call scientific proof is essentially subjective and merely part, a limited part, of gaining knowledge, but without understanding of the whole. Too much reliance is placed upon the limited capacity of logic and reasoning to give any accurate picture of the many faces of reality. This overemphasis upon detail and "proof" has diminished your own ability to feel joy and ecstasy, by destroying trust in your own sensitivity, instincts, and feelings. This has led to a sense of powerlessness and a "victim" consciousness that lowers your vitality. The lack of vital energy has in turn led to many physical problems with the immune system of the body, illness, and hormonal imbalances. The problem is even found in the animal kingdom that reflects what happens to humans. There is an innate need, in all life forms, to experience joy and express it creatively through the physical senses as well as the mind.

Alignment at Kerlescan

If humans, as children or adults, are not given opportunities to explore the creative wealth of the right brain, but confined within the restrictions of an intellectual framework, the result is not simply unfulfilling but censorship of the truth. Some, reacting but not knowing where to turn, try to find consolation in the use of drugs. This leads to an even greater split between the two sides of consciousness; it cannot lead to integration, as the experience is unconnected—not spontaneously achieved—and it limits the possibility of creative development in any grounded way. The present extremes of experience from drug use can result in complete withdrawal from life or in the bizarre manifestation of a demonic force from the subconscious level; whereas the shamans of earlier cultures could directly use their induced experience of environmental forces to enhance their life's work for the community.

Today the uncontrolled use of drugs and alcohol often connects only with the negative aspects of an already confused environment.

If right-brain intuitive creativity were encouraged from birth as a matter of course through childhood education, if it were continued into adult life by the conscious development and refinement of your physical senses of seeing, hearing, touching, smelling, and tasting, there would be a stronger access and commitment to a balanced and creative personal life, more individual responsibility, and more personal independence. You were intended to use your five senses to the full, together with the sixth sense of intuition. All of these combine to make a seventh sense of love, which enables you to find peace in belonging to the universe, and this can be expressed through creative achievements. How rarely do we see this happen now! Yet at one time in the early development of human life, as the indigenous peoples were evolving on Earth, their senses were a total experience. Seeing, hearing, smelling, tasting, and touching were at one with inner knowing. Complete awareness was immediate; there was no room for doubt, as life or death so often depended on an instant response. The senses fragmented and separated as the intellect developed, and feelings suffered by being rationalized. Confusion, doubt, and fear crept in, and many actions were based on those emotions.

Ideally, living through the senses, allowing yourself to be guided by the information you receive, holding it in balance in a mind not confused by negative emotions, you will accept the joys, trials, and challenges of life as a route to the exploration of your own depths and resources.

You were intended to express both your sensitivity and your sensuality through love, so that you move beyond these to higher levels of experience. Denial of either of these gifts is a rejection of a most important instrument for learning as well as a denial of the flow of life. How can you ever be in tune with the cosmos if you are not even in touch with your own sensitivity? A failure to respond with positive sensitivity to life results in hardened emotions, internalized feelings, and many neuroses. If you had been able throughout history to express your sensitivity and creative feelings positively, your emotions would never have become so dark and fearful as we see them today.

There are specific experiences or sensings related to the chakras, which we speak of in more detail later. The higher sensing of the crown chakra encourages freedom of spirit; the sensing of the pineal chakra allows you to trust yourself and not be dominated by others. It also connects you with the intuitive knowing of "the universal mind." The sensitivity of the throat chakra is intended to express the love that comes from the heart. The manifest fullness of the heart is in that expression of feelings of love, and in a loving connectedness to all that is. The receptivity of the solar plexus enables you to be aware of immediate environmental influences and to protect yourself if necessary. The sacral chakra senses creative input and ignites the creative flame that passes through the other main chakras, while the sensing of the base chakra grounds and connects you with the physical world. There will be a new attunement to creative sensitivity in the times to come, and a new harmony in life as a result.

You are actually in the process of learning to become true human beings, fully incarnate, learning to align your personal will to that of the Creator. In doing this your ability to co-create will be developed; even in your own lives you have always been co-creators, for good or ill. You have not always realized that in all situations you have a choice. It is not the Creator who punishes you for deeds that you might regret; the Creator does not judge, but allows. It is humans, you yourselves, who are judgmental, unable to forgive, who punish yourselves and others by choosing repeated lives of suffering until the reasons are forgotten and a pattern is set. We say to you, now it is time to stop the suffering and feel the joy. Start using your ability to sense positively instead of negatively.

By making use of the inner guidance that comes from the Source of all life, you will achieve the highest expression of your own creative talents. When you can free yourselves from the limitations of your religious and educational systems and see beyond emotional restrictions, all possibilities will open up for you; you will be able to express life fully and, in doing so, communicate joy and vitality to others. You have a responsibility to both yourself and the universe to manifest your creative talents, using the six senses that connect you with spirit. Such a shift in consciousness will strengthen your personal integrity and enable you to regain your spiritual identity. But if you fail to make use of these senses positively, you will not evolve beyond a certain stage.

Keeping in close touch with your own sensitivity brings you nearer to the language of the elemental forces of earth in stone, fire, water, the wind, and the clouds. You will become more attuned to the messages of vitality, the subtleties of the life force which, like all living creatures, they contain.

To regain equilibrium with the universe, human beings need to live in conscious harmony with all of nature's other beings on the planet and achieve again the cooperative relationship with them that once existed. Only then can the power of Love be truly manifest on Earth.

The personalities that you have assumed over centuries of distorted self-perception are now in danger of separating you from your soul's destiny. They hold you back. You are in a state of conflict with yourselves, controlled by the tight rein of fear. For humanity this is the final frontier: fear of other life forms both visible and invisible, fear of each other, fear of being sensitive to life. Global disharmony has resulted, evident in the physical and emotional damage of war, civil conflict, and social strife. Attunement is needed, within yourselves and with the Great Spirit, the Creator of ever-changing life.

In times long past, the early forms of civilization were able to acknowledge their people's origins, their seeding from the skies. They honored their ancestors, keeping their memory alive and in ritual returning their souls to the planets and stars whence they had come. Ancestral help and intervention was recognized and accepted in community life, until larger populations and rivalries for land and power led to a culture of fear, a reliance upon sacrifice to the unseen. The gods had to be propitiated. Now the interplay of ancestral energy, with its continual presence which affects your daily lives, is no longer even acknowledged by many of you. We do not mean that your ancestors should be worshiped, but there needs to be an understanding that if they are not at peace, then neither will you be.

Now is the time to find out who your ancestors really are, and how the infinite, orderly world of spirit continues to harmonize with the present incarnation of your soul on its journey through this and every life.

Beating the System

Although access is allowed to one small section of the main alignments at Le Ménec, most of the principal area is now firmly fenced off, visible to the many tourists only from the roadway or a distant viewing platform. By the time we needed to identify the third stone, which we knew was near the ruined cromlech at the eastern end, there was no way in. However, we soon found it was possible to slip between the fencing and the dense undergrowth to where the barrier ended — clearly visitors were not expected to struggle so far — and we could enter the rows. Rather disturbingly, there was a helicopter flying immediately overhead at the time. Hoping no patrolling gendarme would see us, we quickly located the right stone, having been told by one of the others that it was the third from the end in the fourth row. After a consultation with this smaller menhir, and taking one or two photographs, we thanked it, had a look at the others and unobtrusively left by the way we had entered without being arrested.

Previously we had been able to go up to the Giant, stroll around it and sit quietly alongside; this was most important for the work we had to do. Now we realized that another photograph of the Giant was needed, but we could no longer reach it, for, unlike the other, it is in open ground and very visible. Wondering whether to approach the archaeological authorities to obtain permission, I thought of all the likely bureaucratic problems and decided that was not the way.

Natasha and I were driving slowly along the road that runs parallel to the alignments, and as we came abreast of the great monolith I noticed two men in blue jackets by the fence. They were dismantling two of the steel-mesh panels. Seizing the chance, I jumped out of the car and asked if I could go in to take a couple of photos. Yes, was the reply after a moment's hesitation, but be quick. I went in, pressed the shutter button, came out and said thank you very much. No problem, was the answer. This experience was followed by an enormous feeling of gratitude to our invisible friends, knowing that our project was being watched over and the obstacles removed.

—*Hamilton*

CHAPTER 3

Origins

Oh, Adam was a gardener, and God who made him sees
That half a proper gardener's work is done upon his knees,
So when your work is finished, you can wash your hands and pray
For the Glory of the Garden that it may not pass away!
And the Glory of the Garden it shall not pass away.

—Rudyard Kipling

The beautiful garden which was created on Earth has been neglected, because long ago it was subconsciously abandoned by humankind; yet separation from it is a deprivation for the soul. Its restoration depends upon each one of you and your ability to care for it. Re-creation of the Garden will serve to rebuild the aura of your planet that is now clouded by so many negative thought-forms.

The intimacy with nature experienced in a garden which feeds all the senses is not something you can afford to overlook; the inspiration which feeds the soul can be felt there through the senses of touch, taste, smell, hearing, and vision. You can have a feeling of participation in something of creation that is larger than yourself.

Stones at Le Ménec

For the same reason, it is vital for all human beings to experience being part of the Garden of Earth. Yet for so many people who spend their days within enclosing walls, this is no longer central to their life. A conscious return is needed because the Earth, as the original Garden of paradise, is a tangible, visible link in the flow of energy between the higher and lower worlds of spirit. By lower worlds, we do not mean dark or inferior, but those unseen levels of existence which are at a lower stage of evolution than you, and are thus essentially supportive of human life. Higher worlds, also unseen, exist and are committed to advance the evolution of human souls while not necessarily forming part of the evolutionary process. But we have to say that the cosmic connection between these different levels of being is no longer working in alignment with divine intention.

At the same time the flow of vitality from the solar system to Earth is being restricted and interrupted. As a result, the essential supply of cosmic energy is not enough for the present needs of the planet; much of it is being lost or deflected. With appropriate stewardship the Earth's energetic aura would be seen from our perspective to glow with light; but this is not the case.

All this is happening because of the widespread human feelings of separation, the lack of any sense of being part of a greater whole. Behind this sense of alienation is a want of knowledge and understanding of the origins of humanity and your purpose in the totality of existence. If you look up at the planets in your solar system, at the stars and even beyond to distant galaxies, you will see whence all of you have come.

Before the first people had evolved on Earth, before there were animals, the planet was a garden. Plant life flourished. All the elements were present, and the atmosphere was favorable for the creation of further life.

There came an influx of souls from the other planets because creation needed expansion. The life which was possible on other spheres did not provide the experience of intense physical density, nor offer the challenges and restrictions which, as you well know, are imposed by earthly matter. Some of those who came had been close to those experiences but had actually destroyed their own environment and were in search of a new home.

Originally the incoming was only from the planets in your solar system. It was when beings from other galaxies arrived that trouble really began, although there had certainly been some strife among those who had come before.

Most souls from the planets were close to and full of Love for the Creator, a few were not. Even so, it was their task to create further life on Earth. The angels were not present at this time, being called into service later, following the development of the first human beings.

Being wholeness and all-embracing, the power of creation works on Earth by expanding both form and consciousness, developing over time an endless variety of life-forms which can coexist only in the particular atmosphere and conditions of this very special planet of yours. All of the planets and their various inhabitants, of whatever type, go through lengthy and different processes of evolutionary change in their involvement with this diversity before they can finally return to the light of the Creator. As an essential part of that progression, it is important for every soul to experience life on planet Earth.

These souls from the planets worked with light, thought-forms, and the elements as they created the different species of fish, reptiles, insects, birds, and mammals. They then developed the human species out of the forms already in existence, and because they were so full of Love, they were able to program into the human subconscious an eternal link with the Source of creation, and connections with them and their own planetary origins.

After this time, while the human species was developing, there was a further influx of soul-beings from other galaxies that did not have the Love of the Creator in them. They wanted planet Earth for themselves, and created the race of dinosaurs in the hope that it would prevent the further progress of humankind. It was their intention to take over as the exclusive inhabitants.

As you know, the dinosaurs roamed Earth for many millions of years in the time scale of your planet. Nothing could compete with them. The beings from the planets tried to live alongside these great creatures but eventually it was decided that the dinosaurs had to go because they blocked the way for any new life-form. They were not part of the creation plan, since there was no possibility of cooperation with them, as there has been, for instance, with the elephants. They lacked any ability to communicate or interact with other species. There were volcanic eruptions and the dinosaur population did not survive the change of atmosphere. But the beings from the other galaxies remained. Some had beneficial intent and some did not.

Because some souls came from within your own galaxy, and others from distant galaxies, all had the intention of learning to work with the various influences of your solar system.

Over much time the human species evolved, and the atmosphere of the planet grew denser. The souls coming from the other planets originally had light-bodies and were hardly physical at all in your terms, but were of a loose androgynous form. In time, this state of being became insufficiently challenging and the polarization of energies which was occurring on Earth called for a duality of spirit. Accordingly they divided themselves into male and female entities. Having thus split their souls in two, these beings then began to mate with the original human population that they had formed out of the Earth. It was at that point that the search for unity began. Since then, souls on this planet have been searching for their other halves in each successive lifetime. You are the descendants of that first union. You have been here ever since; some other species have not survived. The beings from the other galaxies also chose to reproduce, but only among themselves at first. It was not until much later, when they had become so enmeshed in the physical world that they forgot their own origins, that they chose to interlock their destinies with human life.

The higher intention behind all of this was to learn to work with the energies of this particular solar system. You are being reminded at this moment that these are the energies with which you too have to work. What happened, however, was that nobody learned very much, because in the emotional density of Earth all these beings in human form became confused. All of you became entangled in the ensuing web of karma and there has been a tendency to see only the negative aspects of the archetypal energies that surround and affect you. A desire for domination, for possessions of every kind, became general. Such emotional drives can lead even the higher self, your own raised consciousness, to choose to work with negative energies, and this has always been a great danger for humanity.

You have been here ever since those long-past times, you are your own ancestors and your own heirs, constantly being reborn upon the Earth. This understanding was fundamental to the way of life of all early peoples, and indeed underlies true spiritual understanding today. It has long been accepted by virtually all oriental traditions. You are on a journey of exploration and discovery.

Long, long ago, then, souls from faraway places chose to take on physical bodies in order to encounter life in a dimension different from their own. The purpose behind this exercise was then, as it is now, to return ultimately to the Source of all life with the wisdom gained from many experiences and greater spiritual strength.

The division of souls has had unexpected repercussions because in the quest for the other half, the true aim of eventual return to unity with the Creator has become secondary and even altogether forgotten. Uniting with another part of your soul is not possible until the separate parts have come to equilibrium within themselves, and have balanced their own male and female energies. Only then can there be an integration of the whole.

As these soul entities adapted to the circumstances of Earth, after many diverse experiments in form, beautiful physical bodies were eventually developed. Your personal auric bodies are all that remain of the original bodies of light, which can still be perceived in various ways by some, and actually seen by others. They can reveal information about your lives and state of health. As the dense physical body developed so too did the chakra system, along with the five senses of touch, taste, sight, smell, and hearing. For a while the sixth sense of intuition was largely predominant since it provided the link to the Creator and to the universe, and all life-forms knew then the need for dependence on such an inner connection. Later that connection weakened as trust diminished, except among those few souls who were, and still are, the torchbearers, who have never lost their connection.

As the incoming souls developed in physicality and began to link with the indigenous inhabitants who had been evolved out of the matter of Earth, there came to be a combining of abilities within the human form. The human species had an intimate knowledge of the Earth and its creatures but no spiritual awareness of the higher levels of existence.

These truly indigenous peoples of the planet have all left their bodies; they exist only in spirit in your present time. Some of those remote groups of people who still live in a primitive or tribal way are their descendants. It is to them that you will have to turn for wisdom and guidance in your stewardship of the planet, since they have souls which came from the stars.

In parallel with this emergence of self-conscious humankind, new plant forms were developed in patterns analogous to the human body, so that you could learn to become, as intended, gardeners of the planet and guardians of all its forms. Part of that plan was to create links and similarities between the structures of plants and those of your bodies to provide a series of keys for aiding the growth of spirit and body. Certain plants act as a mirror to the bodily organs and provide a remedy for the ailments which, it was anticipated, would result from the circumstances of physical life. Illness occurs when there is a loss of inner harmony and a weakening of the spirit through separation from the Source. In those early days such problems had not arisen as there was still a close interaction between each soul, the Creator, and your physical environment.

From these pioneer souls there grew in time splendid civilizations, of which Atlantis, the last, was but one. Much has been written and intuitively remembered about this civilization but no physical evidence has yet become available—although there are those who have knowingly found crystals from that time. From our viewpoint, it was felt to be an episode better forgotten; we hoped that a similar stage in the evolution of human life would not be reached again. Although most of the evidence has thus been hidden from your consciousness, the memory of it has always been at work in your subconscious mind. Sophisticated

67

forms of technology came to be developed there, more complex than your present achievements. Atlantis was not the only civilization to evolve at that time, nor as we have said, was it the first. It was the culmination of a series of impressive cultural developments on different parts of the Earth, inspired by the input of souls from the planets, and it flourished for thousands of years. The influence of Atlantis was great and when disharmony took root there it affected other colonies which the Atlanteans attempted to dominate and control. We will tell you something of what followed.

As the shadow of the Fall darkened the minds of certain Atlanteans, experiments took place which were not motivated by the light of the Creator. Their researches overstepped the boundaries of wisdom and the skills that had been developed were misused for personal power, at the expense of the individual freedom of many. Certain individuals chose to manipulate matter to create a slave population with mutations of form, working with the darkness in their minds instead of the wisdom of their divine origin. This was a form of genetic modification, as you now call it and as it exists today, which comes from left-brain dominance and the use of technology without the leavening of common sense or intuitive spiritual guidance. There was a combining of animal and human bodies and hence of their souls. The soul of each animal species is of a simpler nature than the individual human soul, but dependent for its evolution on its relationship with the human species. The basic survival instincts of the animal kingdom did not combine well with the lower human emotions, which had not had time to evolve, and the combination had the effect of lowering the human soul rather than raising that of the animal.

During that lengthy period there was a considerable understanding of the energetic and healing qualities of minerals, a knowledge of the power of sound and vibration and of the effects of form in geometric structures; the biological frameworks of creation were well known. All of these principles were vulnerable to those whose desire for power led to their misuse, in practices going far beyond what had been intended for humankind. Many were opposed to this, but as innocents with no experience of personal confrontation, they were devastated by their inability to stop the experimentation.

It was in this way that genetic manipulation started. The mutated forms that were created by distortion of the life force have caused karmic suffering which has reverberated constantly in your planet's history, as humans have continued to behave in a less-than-human and certainly less-than-animal way. Only now is the final healing possible in a culmination of, and then release from, the suffering that was caused. Yet at this point we see the human race about to make again the same errors and repeat the program of distortion. Artificial genetic changes which mix and alter the living structures of vegetable, animal, mineral, or human forms do not resonate with the true creation patterns and will simply lead to a total breakdown in the evolutionary process and the death of many species.

This experimental work, combining complex genetic manipulation with powerful thought transference, resulted in hybrid creatures that

69

were part human, part animal, reared to serve. They willingly assisted in tasks that were beyond the average human strength. When Atlantis came to its final end some of these creatures fled with their human friends, and since the land you now call Egypt was already a colony of Atlantis, it was there they went. As they could not reproduce themselves they eventually died out, but their former existence is part of many myths—and as you know, a myth is the symbolic survivor of real events.

Souls that incarnate in human form are intended to evolve and learn about the physical restrictions of matter within all its limitations. Any perversion of creative energy can only lead you away from the light of truth and make it harder to follow the way back to the Creator; there are no shortcuts or easy paths.

There were also those who used the power of crystal to control other areas of the planet. The power released was very great, and the Earth would not transform such negativity. As the land masses absorbed the force, they began to break up, and over several thousand years Atlantis destroyed itself. Its chosen direction was one that we could not allow to continue. There were many warnings before the final cataclysm. Some who were prepared fled to other parts of the globe, taking with them the wisdom with which they had been entrusted. Some went to the Basque Country of Iberia, and later to Britain. Some went to South America, others to Egypt, where evidence of their knowledge and technical skills can be found in the numerical and astronomical information that is incorporated in the Great Pyramid's architecture. Although much knowledge is encoded there, there is no access to wisdom; you could say that it is a decoy. The wisdom of the past is held in that greater keeper of mysteries, the Sphinx.

The Sphinx was built long before the final collapse of Atlantis on a place of special power, a major sacred site at which several energy bands meet. Its particular purpose was to preserve important information which would give later generations insight into the origins of life on Earth. At the right moment we intend to introduce a renewed surge of the cosmic energies which enter at that place, to establish a new awareness of the vital connections between the cosmos and the planet, and demonstrate the true meaning of the phrase "as above, so below."

After Atlantis a new beginning had to be made elsewhere for the continued evolution of life. Then there was sufficient time and space to allow that, but this is no longer the case. You are running out of time; many of the evolutionary cycles are coming to an end. We cannot permit you now to become involved in these acts of self-destruction. There will be a time of renewal for the planet, but it will not take the same form as before.

Many souls have absorbed the problems and lessons that resulted from the fall of that powerful civilization, where the energy turned in upon itself and the fail-safe system of the planet went into a mode of self-destruction. Some souls have healed their personal pain through lessons learned in repeated reincarnations. However, there are others who are motivated to do whatever appears to be possible to the human mind, regardless of consequences. They are would-be creators or, shall we say, designers without the moderating and uplifting input of spirit. Their blinkered attitude does not allow them to experience spirit. Although this is their problem and their pain, their work casts a shadow over the illumination that many of you are starting to experience in a wish and intention to align with the true Creator.

It was clear to us at that time that humanity had not evolved to the level where it could be trusted with the spiritual knowledge to which it had access, yet it was vital that such awareness should not be lost. Many of those who fled the destruction were pure in heart and could preserve something of it, but from that point on, it became secret, hidden, to be shared only with those who had proved themselves worthy. Chosen individuals were initiated into the secrets by a priesthood of old knowledge, so that for some time in Egypt there continued to be a high development of culture completely dependent on Atlantean input for its growth. But the shadows which fell over Atlantean minds also affected the priesthood as the human race multiplied and emotions became contaminated by the misuse of power and wealth. A struggle for technical mastery began. The secrecy that came to surround factual scientific knowledge was extended by religion to spiritual matters, since one might have revealed the other, and they became separated.

A long period followed, lasting some thousands of years, when the Earth had to carry a very heavy burden of negative energy. Powerful, adversarial thought-forms from Atlantis persisted and prevented the furthering of progress of the human soul or physical body. There was a period of stagnation in many areas of the planet. The spiritual darkness was followed by a time of physical darkness that resulted from the cat-aclysmic destruction of Atlantis and its enveloping clouds of dust. There was much loss of life, animal and human, and little vegetation remained. However, there were survivors and life continued, but in a very different way. Spiritual energy was not able to penetrate, as the ability to distinguish between what was true and what was false was not developed sufficiently. The human family had to carry a cursed inher-itance that both preceded and followed Atlantis. Moreover, the inter-breeding of those spirits who came from the planets with those who had evolved from the physicality of planet Earth did not always pro-duce harmonious results. The indigenous people did not have a chakra system such as you have today and this made the absorption of spiri-tual energies difficult, often with negative and reactionary results. Instead of the integration of the forces of spirit and matter, as was the highest intention, there was opposition and further separation.

Those Atlanteans had a very long life span compared to yours now. They were able to live for several hundred years, and many rein-carnated amongst the people of the new lands and intermarried with them. They preserved some of their knowledge and special gifts, becoming teachers of agriculture and of certain arts, such as weaving, music, pottery, architecture, and healing with plants. They shared their knowledge of the stars and of life which had originated in the skies, but never revealed the technology that had been developed in Atlantis. Eventually, as a little more light penetrated the souls of those amongst whom they were living, in parallel with a warmer climate and clearer atmosphere, there came the appropriate time for a more conscious acknowledgment and sharing of the understanding they had brought. Accordingly they began marking out the energy points—the places of power which we had already established—so that they could be recognized and consciously used by humankind. There was a new input at this time from the planets and many souls came to be reborn among those who were already upon the Earth.

When the time comes for humans to become truly human, the ancient knowledge will stir again in your minds and will be shared with all. Nevertheless, knowledge is of value only if it is combined with intuition; then it has the correct alchemy to become wisdom, and can be used in the establishment of a new world for you. Then spirit will truly combine with matter to express the Creator's joy in what has been created.

Over the millennia which followed the Atlantean resettlement in other places, peoples of varying origins and backgrounds spread themselves more widely and migrated northward as weather conditions slowly improved. The growing of crops and the domestication of animals became possible in the most favorable areas. Trading relationships developed between different groups of people and in time those who were to become the megalith builders, traveling by sea and river around the coasts, peacefully occupied the western fringes of the European continent. There they met with other souls who had also hailed from Atlantis. From them they learned the necessity of marking the sacred sites with standing stones to focus and hold the currents of cosmic vitality, anchoring and structuring them to support a more settled way of life. They learned to observe the planetary cycles and honor their own origins, which at that time had not been wholly forgotten. This placement of the stones, which were often aligned to the most significant solar and lunar events of the year, as well as marking a place of power, was intended to ensure that cosmic intelligence would be grounded in earthly wisdom, thereby preventing a recurrence of the Atlantean problems. In this there was an angelic input, as we were able to communicate with the minds of the megalith builders; they were instructed from "on high," as you would say.

There followed a period of stability, of living with integrity and integration, of honoring natural rhythms. Then the priorities of life changed once more, for with the growth of population the link with natural forces was gradually superseded by concern for defending the tribe, its lands, and its livestock. Rivalries developed, tribal boundaries and chieftain leaderships were established. Ritual celebration for the ancestors, ceremonies to honor the Sun or Moon, still continued in the tradition of each locality. As long as there was no shortage of land for hunting and for pasture and primitive crops as static farming replaced the old nomadic way of life, trading and peaceful exchange remained more characteristic of those times than fighting.

The original acceptance and oneness with the abundance of nature faded eventually because there was a subconscious memory of the earlier devastation. The climate began to change, becoming wetter and colder. There was much fear of a recurrence of disaster but without the understanding of what had happened or why. Trust gave way to fear, which was encouraged by those who saw it as a means of control, and so it was replaced by a more apprehensive attitude in which sacrifice, the propitiation of unseen forces or gods, became part of the accepted rituals. Your image of the Creator became fearsome instead of benevolent, and the darkness crept back into human life.

We saw then that technical advance in the use of metals brought with it weapons and intercommunity strife. Warlike panoply became the mark of a tribal leader, and masculine dominance became fully established. As the European climate deteriorated, much land became unsuitable for cultivation and competition for territory took the place of peaceful cooperation. Soon old ceremonies were put aside; land-hungry peoples from the East encroached on small farming communities in successive waves of migration. The struggle for power over both nature and other people was once again under way and has continued ever since.

Increasingly, those with the ability to receive higher guidance through divination of various kinds were pressed into revealing it. In this there was an element of coercion so that information was not always received or given clearly. These divinatory practices became dangerous for all concerned since guidance was not willingly given at times of need, rather, it was demanded for political ends and individual satisfaction. The minds of those who were oracles, at Delphi and Dodona for example, became disturbed and open to the influence of a consciousness that was lacking in divine content. Guidance became limited, sometimes malevolent, and usually cryptic. All divination, or channeling, eventually fell into disrepute and until recent times has been surrounded by fear and superstition.

Divination, when its truth can be perceived, will give you another perspective on your life. It can show how the past shapes the present, enabling you to work consciously to create the future. All human beings have the ability to connect with the higher part of themselves and so gain access to the reality of the soul's journey; many can go higher and make contact with the mind of the universe. These are your mystics, whose purpose it is to seek higher truths and so raise the level of human consciousness. Their insight has been earned through many incarnations of working with an intuitive mind, balanced by an understanding of spiritual law and the cosmic process.

The deviation from natural law, or what you know as the Fall, did not first occur on the Earth; it happened in the world of spirit in the earliest days long before humanity's physical development. All that takes place in the physical world of matter is but a reflection of what has already happened in spiritual realms. As above, so below; the physical is always a manifestation of the state of the spirit.

Already in being, the higher worlds of the angels accepted certain responsibilities, including the guidance and planned development of life on Earth. But the angels were themselves influenced by the polarities of the physical environment, and duality entered our ranks. The highest angelic and also human quality is the surrender of personal will to that of the Creator. Although our energies are a neutral force in the universe, dual aspects developed in the nature of each angel. It is for humanity to recognize and choose to work with the positive power of light or the negative energy of darkness. We are neutral since we serve only the Creator, and as all that exists is an aspect of the Creator, even the darkness ultimately will be turned to the light. But now there is an opposition—the will of the dark against the will of the light, or the will of the lowest against that of the highest. That was the first separation in the heavens, which has been reflected ever since on Earth as human life developed.

It was realized, however, that this division or conflict of energy could be used to test the strength of the connection between Creator and that which was created, so that ultimately it too would be of service. Nevertheless the darkness would intervene in the human life which was to evolve on Earth, and affect, to the extent possible, all earthly events. As these intentions led to the creation of an entity in the world of spirit, the next step was to find a material vehicle for it so that it could be processed and transformed by future life-forms on their own level. Your angelic guides selected the vehicle of the human left brain for this function.

The gift of intelligence is thus both your demon and your angel. It can also be the route to conscious awareness. If you can be intelligent without becoming overly intellectual, you may have access to wisdom. The intellectual mind, however, tends to deny the Creator, lacking access to the intuitive wisdom of the right brain and vainly seeking proof which can come only through true feeling and empirical knowledge. The limited thinking that comes from a left brain insufficiently connected with the right brain can also lead to negative emotional responses. So it is through these negative emotions that you access the dark or lower aspects of our angelic attributes.

The human mind has been a tool of the darker forces who knew what potential was there. When the personal experience of mystical union with the cosmos, such as the Gnostics had, was discredited by religious doctrines, it left a void in the mind that longed for nourishment. This longing made it possible for any belief system to be installed. Direct spiritual experiences were not encouraged, called pagan and heretical, and were even punishable by death. This eliminated the trust in intuitive personal guidance and cut the connection between the Creator and the creation. It was in this way that the human mind developed belief systems, each of which professes to be the only way, but each of which has been the cause of so much human suffering.

Logic exists only in the earthly realm, nowhere else in the solar system, although there are elements of it in other realms of the universe. It is part of the human illusion fostered since the days of Aristotle. Those who try to live by logic and rationality alone will find themselves very uncomfortable in the higher worlds of spirit, just as will those who are ruled by the emotions and by systems of belief.

In the etheric worlds of spirit, the energy of darkness drew a veil over the light and took the form, as it were, of a dragon. Although dragons

Stone at St. Pierre-Quiberon

have never existed in your physical world, there have certainly been people who have seen their etheric image; an actual physical presence would have allowed them an unbalanced sense of power.

One dragon that you all know well is the internal saboteur. This dragon encourages you to continue opposing the natural flow of life, making decisions which are the opposite of divinely inspired, and so prolonging your suffering. In your mythology, which always contains elements of the truth, this dragon has a reputation for devouring maidens; this may be seen as a subconscious, symbolic representation of feminine intuitive wisdom being overcome by the masculine intellect of the left brain.

Another dragon, we can say, is guardian of a treasure. If you can get past this dragon of the intellect you will gain access to the treasures of wisdom.

In the time to come, the maiden, as in the myth, will be rescued at the eleventh hour—this is the point that we see humanity has now reached—by the sword of light wielded by the Archangel Michael. It is Michael who can tame the power of the dragon and have a balancing influence upon the twin hemispheres of the human brain. Since the original Fall from a state of Grace, the separation of intellect from intuition is expressed in your lack of balance between masculine and feminine energies, between the dark and the light; but these dualities and the feelings of alienation from the Creator and from the Garden are in truth illusory. Your present challenge is to unite these elements and start to live in harmony with the positive truth of their unity.

The Fall did not affect the animal, plant, and mineral kingdoms directly. They remained in a state of Grace, although this is much affected by your activities, since they are influenced by human thought and can absorb human negativity. Domestic animals, for example, will often take on an illness of their owner, helping to bear the burden. Trees and plants will become stunted or deformed if the Earth's vibrations are disturbed or if their planetary links are interrupted by human agency. Crystals too can absorb negative energy just as they can be programmed for higher, more positive frequencies.

There is a story in the Sufi tradition that illustrates the Fall and its influence upon the Earth. A Sultan asks his court magician for an apple, a perfect apple. The magician produces the apple and the Sultan, taking a bite, finds a maggot in it. When he demands an explanation, the magician tells him that the apple was perfect until it entered Earth's atmosphere, where it became contaminated by negative energy. All life on the Earth has been subject to such negative influences. There is not one arena in life in which the darkness has not been present at some time, and this affects those at all social levels. The apple too has a deeper significance, as it represents the knowledge that has also become contaminated.

When Love is present all such negativity can be transformed; but in Love's absence it will be amplified.

The plant and animal realms support and are in service to humankind in many ways, and depend for their evolutionary progress on appropriate interaction with humanity and one another. Therefore, they are to be respected and nurtured always. They do not comprehend the suffering you so casually inflict on them by way of scientific experimentation or in the production of food for your consumption. If you are responsible for causing suffering to an animal then, on a soul level, you are inviting that energy into your own life, and you will experience what you are causing. If an animal has been slaughtered in a state of fear, that fear becomes part of your food. When the vegetables you eat are chemically treated, unfeelingly handled in factories, and transported long distances, the original nourishment is dissipated and cannot reach you. And if you eat food that has not been blessed, you are at the mercy of its vibrations of whatever kind.

On the other hand, when food is blessed before being eaten, its vibrations are raised to a higher level before it enters your body; you transform any negative energy that has accumulated in it so that it can do you no harm. If you bless yourself too, so that you are in a state of Grace when you eat, the food will enhance what is highest in you and will not feed negative emotions such as greed. Eating will then be a positive experience, nourishing body and soul and simultaneously conferring a grace upon what is consumed.

Once there was widespread human understanding of these concepts. There was much expression of light in the positive honoring of all created things. For a while there was harmony, because there was the intention to work with the combination of spirit and matter up to its highest potential, until the dragon power was realized and certain individuals began to feel its influence. Not honoring spirit or matter and

83

desiring only to manipulate, they started the process of destruction. In that way the original innocence was threatened in order to be strengthened at a later period, but at that time failed to meet the challenge.

There is a warning for you in those forgotten parts of your history. Because you have distorted and failed to learn from the teachings of every master who has taken on human form to remind you of your task on Earth, there has been no re-creation of the earthly paradise of which they spoke. While this might have been possible in the earliest days of Atlantis, it was not to be achieved in the long and laborious rebirth of world cultures that followed its destruction.

Because of the Earth changes to come, many of you will be directed into a more natural lifestyle than is presently experienced. This time it is essential that the changes be accompanied by a real connection with the guidance of the soul force within you. You will need to find ways to work together which exclude habits of devious manipulation and reactionary emotional behavior, in order to experience harmony within yourselves, with each other, and with all other forms of life. You will find it necessary to keep in touch with the elemental and angelic realms; only then will you be able to restructure your patterns of living on Earth and create a planet of paradise. Only then will you return to the Garden and live, as intended, in harmony with the material and spiritual gifts which your planet, within the framework of the solar system, has to offer in such abundance.

A sensitive attunement to spiritual laws will enable you to create a balance between what needs to be brought forward and what needs to be left behind; there is very little in your present culture that truly inter-acts with the highest spirit. There will be a new culture, based upon a relationship with other realms, along with an awareness and celebration of the rites of passage of the soul's journey. There will be a new under-standing of the significance of planetary cycles and influences. These observances will free the spirit, as opposed to past religious doctrine that has imprisoned it in teachings of judgment and punishment. There will be a reawakening to the truth. Earth will become a sanctuary where shame, humiliation, and cruelty are not known.

A number of those souls who left their bodies at the ending of the Atlantean civilization chose not to incarnate in human form. Instead, they came back as dolphins, so as to remain in service to the Creator and remind their fellow humans of the essence of spirit, which is joy. These souls had observed how easily humans can fall from Grace and deny or forget their origins. They did not ever want to forget, so they chose a form in which they could help to foster the essential balancing power of Love. Dolphins are a pure form of Creator essence, embody-ing a love and wisdom that they wish to share with you. Some of you have experienced the feelings of joy that come from an encounter with them, sometimes followed by sorrow that such love is so rarely found in human relationships.

Now these souls are exercising choice once more, returning to human form and so bringing that love directly into human life. Many children being born in all parts of your world have had a previous life as a dolphin, and now, out of water, they may have a difficult time learning about physical life in your element. Much has changed since they were last among you; they will need a lot of support and understanding, as they will seem very pure and not at all worldly-wise. But having great clarity of mind, these children will grow up to reveal to you many of the ancient secrets. For dolphins are among those who have retained that knowledge, and now, through their characteristic of love, it can be attained to help humanity move out of darkness and once more into the light.

Death of an Owl

Traveling in France one day, Hamilton and I made a detour along the valley of the Loire and decided to visit the ancient Abbey of Fontevraud. The Abbey was once an important center of wisdom and learning, attended by many famous and distinguished people. It is the burial place of Henry II, king of England (whose first language was French); his queen, Eleanor of Aquitaine; and their son, Richard Coeur de Lion, also a king of England. Restoration of the buildings was in progress and for us it was a symbolic setting, yet another reminder of much-needed restoration elsewhere.

We walked in the cool light through spacious rooms with pale stone walls and flagstone floors, then entered the Abbey church, tall and dark, where lie the royal tombs, painted and emblazoned. Eventually we went outside into the sunlit and beautiful gardens, with green lawns and neatly trimmed hedges. Turning off the path to see the roses, while no one was about, we saw something white lying on the grass. The pure white on green was startling, for white stands for purity and green is the color of the full heart. Moving closer, we saw soft feathers and realized it was a small owl, a barn owl that looked to be dead.

Hamilton picked it up with care. As he gently held it, its eyes opened, it looked at us both for a moment, then closed its eyes and died. We laid it among the roses.

It shared something with us, who witnessed its leaving. The owl is an old and familiar symbol of wisdom. It is a bird that flies in the darkness so as to keep wisdom alive through the darkest times, and it always keeps a watchful eye on life. In the skies it reminds us not only of whence we came, but also that wisdom will take us back there.

The owl, in its actual death, stands for a more general death, the loss of awareness in human beings of the significance of other dimensions of being, other kingdoms of life. The old shamanic connection with all natural forms is dying too.

The incident stirred us, for we realized that the owl was a messenger to us from the consciousness of the universe. At death it returned to another world, a higher level of owl consciousness, and perhaps back to a greater wisdom than ours. Its dying made clear that we had taken on certain responsibilities—to reawaken the ancient wisdom by accessing the Archangels' message in the stones and to keep alive a vision of divine unity. We needed to become more receptive to signposts by the wayside, to learn the meaning of synchronicity and how it affects our perceptions, and explain to others the potential of working with all our unseen friends.

—Natasha

CHAPTER 4

Grace

We are all of us in the gutter, but some of us are looking at the stars.

—Oscar Wilde

As the Archangels, we are the bearers of Grace, the Grace of the Creator. We have observed for some time that the human race has lost its dignity and has entered a process of decline. Accordingly we bring you this concept of Grace as part of the divine intention to restore both dignity and Grace to all of you.

Grace is a quality that has been lacking since the human descent into materialism and the dominance of the intellect. It is the means by which you can bring back the magic that informs all life movement and makes all things possible. Grace is Love, Grace is honoring, Grace is dignity. Some of you say a "grace" before a meal, but unless you feel it in your heart with love, really giving thanks *to* the food, not *for* it, and so turn it into a blessing upon what you eat and upon yourself, the act remains on the mental or intellectual level. It has no effect unless combined with feeling.

If you had 100 percent focused attention in each moment, you would act only with Love, and every action in your life would be full of Grace. It is the attachment to the past and fear of the future that makes people act out their shadow emotions, setting up more tensions in the present. Yet to live in the present requires constant vigilance and an extended awareness of what is happening beyond your immediate visual surroundings. You must link up with the messengers of Grace, who can help you to extend your sensitivity and awareness. When you are filled with the Grace of wisdom, you have the power to take appropriate action for the highest good, for both yourself and others.

The human physical body operates with the vibrational energies of solar, cosmic, and earthly origin. Since its actions are in part the response of your emotional and mental bodies to those vibrations, learning to respond to them with Grace will be an essential quality of a true human being of the future.

We are well aware that it is difficult for you to feel a state of Grace when most of you think that you are carrying burdens that cannot be laid down or surrendered. The Grace of the Creator has the power to heal all old wounds through the acceptance of them as necessary learning experiences, which, although you may find it difficult to believe, are of your own choosing. All of these experiences can be integrated into your life and used to loosen the constraints that hold you back. The acceptance of them has to happen before any effective healing can take place. Healing may not be obvious. It may be an inner change that is perceived only in an altered behavior or attitude. Healing is an assignment with Grace itself, allowing and enabling the self to become a channel for Love, which in turn reaches you through our angelic help. Without our presence it cannot take place. Many people whose way of life has made them sick have experienced healing by restoring a sense of Grace to their lives and recovering it in themselves. By establishing a new connection between their own inner rhythms and the force of Love, they have revitalized themselves, and by taking responsibility for their own healing they have not only cured themselves but also learned why the illness came about and what it had to teach them. Illness can be a great teacher, and when human intentions are informed with Love, then the miracle can occur.

There are diverse and valid forms of healing which are presently favored and many more waiting to be discovered for future use. There were once temples in Greece where color healing was understood and practiced. It was known, too, by early aboriginal and other ethnic peoples that the various tonalities of sound can redistribute energies within and outside the body. Both of these forms of healing have been revived and are used today within your modern civilization, but only by a minority who understand something of them. They can be used negatively also, and as you may know, some of your scientists have made studies of the negative and destructive effects of certain frequencies of sound as well as the benefits. The effects of color on the human psyche, which is so sensitive to light, are also being well researched.

Crystals, too, can draw out negative energy, but they can also focus it. The ability to work with any form of energy for healing requires Grace. All forms of healing exist to realign the conscious mind and to remind the body of its blueprint of perfection and so reopen you to the possibility of wholeness. Too often both sound and color are used only to manipulate mood and influence for commercial ends, rather than for creating a healing environment.

Dolmen at Mané Kerioned

Sadly, the essential component of Grace has been removed from much of your current medical practice. Particularly in the West, it has become excessively rational (what you are accustomed to call scientific), losing in the process its intuitive aspect. If your doctors learned to diagnose in ways similar, in principle at least, to the shamans of old—who could tune in to the individual patient's needs and feel the vibrations of an appropriate medicine or treatment—then they would feel a greater empathy with the real needs of the patient. In consequence, a more sympathetic and effective healing could take place. Chemically produced drugs, now so routinely prescribed for every ailment, lack the essential life force. Often they effect too powerful a physical change in the sensitive human body. Further medication is required to counteract the damage, thus starting a cycle of dependency. Unfortunately your medical profession has lost much of its traditional integrity and has, perhaps unwittingly, compromised itself to the commercial and chemical worlds, to the industries that are willing to perpetuate illness for commercial gain. These priorities will change as people return to a more naturally balanced attitude toward health, with greater sensitivity to sickness in the individual and the use of less invasive treatments.

Experiencing a sense of Grace aligns you with your purpose and makes you feel centered. Standing foursquare in life and balanced spiritually, mentally, emotionally, and physically, you can avert possible problems by knowing what actions to take, and what actions to avoid. In this our archetypal qualities are always available to you, helping to arrange the circumstances needed for the growth of your spirit, for we and the angelic host have long been the overseers of life on Earth. If your personality is in conflict with your soul's destiny, then you may find yourself changing course rather dramatically, perhaps without having made a conscious decision to do so; it is we who will have intervened on behalf of your higher self.

Many of you are like warriors weary of the battle, having fought your way through centuries of delusion, now needing to summon courage for the last fight. As in the stories of King Arthur, questing knights in their dented armor are starting to clear a way through the thickets of belief and disbelief, allowing light to enter the forest of illusion, chasing away old nightmares. With our help, the forest can be opened up to the light of Love by Grace, which has the power to diminish the density of the material world.

Old fears and inhibiting systems of belief have diverted you from the experience of Grace and closed your minds to spiritual influence, separating you from life's purpose and fulfillment. From now on, each one of you has to take responsibility for your own development, letting yourself be guided wisely by the light of Love and showing compassion for all life.

Much of the stress on your planet is due to the excessive and continuous flood of diverse information from your various methods of communication, what you call the media; they are impressive vehicles for transmitting the darker aspects of the archetypal energies. They spread fear and alarm with ease, thriving on sensation. Yet there has always been some form of stress, always some oppression that creates clouds of negativity around humanity which other souls have had to work hard to counteract. In the past the monks of Tibet and other remote places made efforts to keep the presence of Grace on the planet through their chanting and devotions. These activities by isolated groups are now becoming less necessary as consciousness is raised and you as individuals become responsible for charting your own destinies, finding your own way, free from the limitations that old beliefs have set around your minds.

It is time for human beings to become truly human and fully incarnate upon the planet. Then and only then can there be fulfillment of soul destiny. Then you will understand the cosmic laws of order. The law of plenty, for example, holds that it is possible for there always to be enough, but this cannot be so unless something is given in return for what has been received, giving the Earth time to restore itself when you have harvested its fruits. The law of attraction states that people and events are drawn to you by unconscious links, to help you to fulfill their destinies and your own. There are other laws which you will discover as we work with you.

You have never been fully incarnate in this world, as all your lives have been fragmentary, leaving parts—attachments—in other dimensions of spirit without your conscious awareness. This is the time to integrate the fragments, pulling all the learning from each incarnation into this present life, taking personal responsibility for the creation of a new environment which will be healthy and nourishing for all, accepting that your soul is eternal and, for its evolution, has to be free to move on at its separation from the body at the time of physical death.

Not all of your incarnations have been filled with negative experiences. Some have brought you joy, fulfillment, the graceful learning of skills; these are the completed, well-polished fragments of the soul. It is those lives that were unfulfilled, that still carry unresolved trauma and lessons unlearned, which cause difficulties in your present life, difficulties which we are concerned to help you overcome.

You actually live in a magical universe where the power of thought combined with feeling is the strongest tool that has ever existed, for good or ill. When thought is dominated by fear, it invites in the powers of darkness and creates weapons of darkness. Some of you who have experienced pain in love and have had illusions swept aside to reveal a difficult truth have become afraid of the power of love, fearing that it may yet cause you further pain. Instead you find solace in sentimentality, a shallow form of emotional closeness. The most effective form of alchemy has not always been present to provide the key to a joyful life. But when thought is governed by selfless love, miracles can and do happen; this too is a law of the universe.

As inhabitants of this special planet, you need a new focus for your thoughts, one which is not directed only toward the material aspects and acquisitions of living. These things are not to be ignored, but their overemphasis leads to further imbalances, in the health of both the individual and the environment as a whole. Your materialistic society is addicted to acquisition and sentimentality, and any addiction, whether material or spiritual, means that you are not in control of your own life. Addiction is a substitute for something you need to experience on another level. You are more likely to be thrown entirely off center by any force stronger than yourself that you have failed to take into account and the potential beauty of life will continue to evade you. If, for example, you are addicted to control and you insist on trying to control circumstances or the people around you, you lose control of your own life. This is a denial of the existence of a higher order, the order that arranges the flow of life. It is much easier to work with it than against it. Life becomes more of an adventure in this way and lets in a more spontaneous energy.

To free yourself from such limitations, make use of the power that lies within your own intuitive mind and renew the link with the inner teacher who can be found there. This will give you new support to your life, one which will help you to keep your head above water when circumstances change or the tide seems adverse. Your inner teacher can lead you to an all-embracing empathy with the environment, in the state of Grace which recognizes its awesome beauty. These wonderful qualities will be fully appreciated through getting to know, love, and value your planet, more than ever before in its history. Many of you have been reduced to the role of tourists, complacent onlookers, detached from the Earth's vitality and variety, and above all from its significance in the evolution of the human soul. A mere visual connection to the wonders of the planet is not enough.

Those of you who live in the cities can take yourselves to the parks and sit under the trees. Listen to what the trees have to say—it may surprise you. Fill your homes with plants so that their energy can activate the Grace of healing in your daily life and revitalize the air you breathe.

When life lacks vitality, gracefulness, and fulfillment, it is because you are in a state of denial, closed in some way to so many possible sources of spiritual nourishment, oblivious even of their very existence and your need of them. You are only half alive, partially frozen, unable to sing your own songs like the birds, because of your doubt that you are meant to be truly yourselves. It does not serve the Creator to be less than you truly are.

Your life on Earth will be so different with the realization of why you are here and where you came from; how you were carefully prepared in the worlds of spirit for this incarnation by those who truly love you. When a child is born into your world, it has usually come from a place of deep, blissful Love in a world of spirit. It cries because it now needs to find that same Love in the physical world, and it is that otherworldly Love that so many souls are subconsciously nostalgic for, as no human love is able fully to replace it.

Your life is not a chance occurrence. It has been deliberately arranged for your benefit through your cosmic connections. It is for you to see this and feel it. Work positively with these connections and they will work for you, work against them and disharmony will follow. There are always opportunities and choices to be made which determine the quality of your life. Learn to see the signposts and act accordingly.

Each of you made a contract with your soul before incarnating. With the traumas of birth and entry into an alien and often unloving society, your contract has been forgotten, but its validity does not cease to hold. It will continue to direct the course of your life. The contract ensures that you are always connected with the Grace of the Source, even though the vibrations of fear that arise in later life do not always allow you to feel it.

We are always with you. Your souls are vast entities that reach far into the universe; they are not trapped inside the body. Your soul projects a part of itself into each earthly incarnation and thus breathes spirit into matter. Even while your personality or ego can keep you strongly attached to the physical body, your soul may be conversing with the angels. The soul holds the blueprint of your full potential for the present incarnation. How you interpret this blueprint is for you to decide, and the way in which you combine human qualities and our Archangelic attributes is for you to choose.

Sometimes it may seem easier to resist the flow of inner guidance and follow the dictates of society, morality, or convention. You may feel it would be crazy to go against this comfortable arrangement— until you realize that it represents the certain stagnation of the soul. As your spirit grows it becomes less comfortable with compromise. If you do not follow your true destiny, the spirit starts to withdraw and you start to separate yourself from Grace.

At times in your lives it is important and appropriate to give help to others. At other times, doing so will remove the opportunity for them to find their own strength and self-esteem by helping themselves. It is the Grace of discernment that tells you when to help and when to hold back. When help is not appropriate, it will not be well received, and may indeed be given conditionally in a way that will later cause resentment. In that event it can do more harm than good. This applies to our angelic help, as well as in human-to-human help. The true gift of helping is the right kind of help at the right time. You have a saying that the angels help only those who help themselves, and this is true. Our qualities can empower you, but the first move is always yours.

Our challenge for you is to succeed in raising your self-esteem and regain your lost dignity by learning to live in the Grace and celebration of your environment and of one another's gifts. You will do this by helping yourselves to fulfill your aspirations creatively, and by developing an intuitive rapport with the wisdom within your own souls.

Be graceful, loving, and wise in all things.

Footprints of the Angels

For many years now geometric patterns have been appearing in the fields of standing crops in Britain and in other countries such as France and Canada. The number of patterns has been increasing, the designs are becoming more complex, but their origin and meaning remain obscure. These large and puzzling symbols have come to be known as crop circles, and most are now recorded by aerial photography. While initial interest from the media has faded, there is enthusiasm from a growing band of investigators. This has caused some farmers to get in the combine and remove the markings as quickly as possible before the public arrives and perhaps tramples the crop.

We are given to understand that they are a reminder of other dimensions, impressed upon the ground by an angelic force, and it is apparent that some represent the stars, the planets, and the pattern of their motions as we see them in the sky. They are also quite jokey, indicating that we humans are not the only ones with a sense of humor. Above all, they are injections of higher energy.

The angels have long been specially interested in the region around Avebury, the immense stone circle in southern Britain with its dolmens and smaller circles, where a wide solar band and the Christ-lines—Michael and Mary—cross and recross at nodal points. A stone avenue actually marks the precise course of the Michael line, while the Mary line takes in the mysterious mound of Silbury Hill. Not a summer passes but numerous crop circles appear in the area. (Photographs of these appear on pages 102 and 127.)

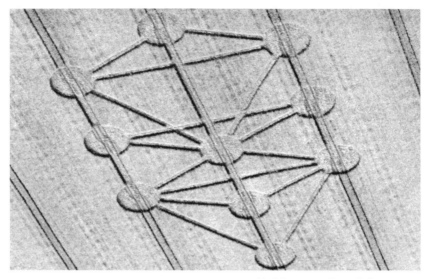

Kabbalah crop circle, Wiltshire 1997
COURTESY OF LUCY PRINGLE

In the photo above, the representation, impressed over the farmer's tractor tramlines, is of the Kabbalist's tree of life, complete with the ten Sefiroth or containers of creative light upon three pillars, with equilibrium at the center, and contraction and expansion on either side. Each Sefira stands for one of the divine attributes, the particular archetypal quality of each Archangel and the corresponding planet. It is a dynamic model of our world as part of the universal energies that are basic to life in every form, visible and invisible. We could hardly expect a more direct reference to the angels' powerful presence and constant availability for humanity. Study the photograph; you will see it is an ancient symbol that may spark certain feelings of recognition.

—Hamilton

CHAPTER 5

The Archangels and the Planets

All culture originates in the spiritual world, that is where the plan-ets are formed, and they in turn determine the course of our lives on the physical plane. The beings who, as we ascend, are closest to human beings are known . . . as angels, Archangels, and prime movers or prime beginners.

—Rudolph Steiner

The dynamics of all human life are inherited from the Archangels, and we, the Archangels, were ourselves formed from the matter of the planets, called into being by the Creator. The archetypal resonance that we share with you comes, in turn, from our association with the indi-vidual planets of the solar system.

By explaining some of our connections with those planets and with you, we hope to raise your feelings of self-worth and offer a view-point which will enable you to open up your hearts and flourish. Each of us has a unique quality or attribute which is to be used in human life. Actually humans have no other choice but to work with these influences, but many of you have developed hardened attitudes that have restricted your ability to do so in a life-enhancing manner.

As Archangels we work as a unity, but it is our individual contributions which need to be positively integrated into your lives to bring inner strength and balance. What hinders the growth of the human soul, more than anything else, is judgment of self and of others. In previous incarnations, so many of you have experienced harsh judgments—under the cloak of religion—that have afflicted your perception of the true nature of spiritual reality. To improve that perception and raise the vibrations of planet Earth and one another, you need to be fully aware, not only of your connections with us, but of our contract with the Creator, which is to assist in all aspects of human life.

The resonances and influences of which we speak reach you by means of planetary emanations, rays if you prefer the term, laid upon Earth in the form of global networks or grids, that we shall attempt now to explain as simply as possible. Your planet is surrounded by this complex web of external planetary energies which are not visible except with the inner spiritual eye, but may be felt and identified by using your dowsing sense perception. The Sun, in particular, and each planet, casts its net as a part of that web of energies, and so each projects on to Earth its own special influence. These energies are distinct from the gravitational forces which hold your solar system together and from other radiations such as the electromagnetic spectrum from the Sun.

Each one of these networks (some of a regular gridlike pattern, others without apparent regularity), is a dynamic field of energy which corresponds to and incorporates the individual attribute of an Archangel, thus enabling the distinctive electromagnetic vibrations of each of us to be carried around the globe. Our archetypal characteristics, thus projected, are the raw material—the spiritual qualities—which you as individuals use to weave your emotional lives on Earth.

The frequency levels of the human brain, tending to fluctuate between one quarter Hertz and some 30 Hertz, or cycles per second, are very much lower than our own. As such, you do not perceive our energy fields, nor see the planetary networks which carry them with the physical eye. In the same way, you do not readily perceive the field of gravity, nor the many electromagnetic fields that increasingly impinge upon you. You are effectively tuned to your own planet at around 8 cycles per second, the optimum frequency of what you term the Schumann Wave which pulses over the Earth's surface. We are tuned to our own angelic realm at higher frequencies, far beyond the scale of which you are currently aware, but able to reach down into yours and see you with our spiritual eyes.

These solar and planetary fields of our angelic energy are not static, but dynamic; at the present time they are in a process of change and it would be misleading to set out more precise definitions in the manner so dear to your scientific profession. There are further layers of cosmic energy fields as vibratory influences from the stars which also affect the Earth, but for now it is sufficient to acknowledge the primary forces coming from the solar system. The flexibility of these influences allows all the benign forces of Creation to be ever present in your world.

The Energetic Nets

The first and most important of these influences comes not from a planet, but from the Sun, the bright star at the center of your solar system. We have already spoken of the megaliths and something of their purpose. Most of them stand upon the solar net—known to many of you as the leyline system—which is an intricate network of energy bands, apparently straight alignments linking the sacred places. These sites, recognized as places of power by your ancestors in the distant past, were honored by them with formal groups of timber uprights or standing stones. Many of the sites have been subsequently occupied by places of worship, the temples, mosques, and churches of your various religions in different parts of the world. Some of these bands of solar energy are very wide and form great circles around the globe; many others are of lesser length and dimension. They surround Earth, anchored to it at certain places of power, and are detectable upon and above it during the hours of daylight. Each band consists of a number of parallel impulses according to its width.

The principal function of this system is to carry the essential life force of the Sun for the material needs of Earth and its animal, vegetable, and mineral kingdoms. This was why early peoples marked and wished to enhance such significant places, for they knew that all fertility, and hence their survival, depended upon the well-being and vitality of those realms of nature and upon the daily presence of the Sun itself.

It was our welcome duty, long ago, as overseers of life on Earth, to establish these places for the inflow of solar power.

At a later stage we found it necessary to create a second network of incoming energy using your largest planet, Jupiter. This was to carry, for humanity's benefit, the vibrations of Love, in order to empower the unification of male and female qualities whose balance was being lost, and to demonstrate and hold for you the transforming power of the Christ consciousness to come. This network consists of two separate but interweaving and curving bands, one of positive polarity, the other of negative polarity. You will realize their importance when we say that they can be found at the Avebury stones and at Glastonbury in England, at Le Mont-Saint-Michel in France, at Delphi in Greece, and at other such well-known places of ancient sanctity upon your globe, where they intersect not only with each other but also connect with the principal solar bands. There are many single branches of each of the twin Jupiter lines, which can be detected at certain important sites such as Gavrinis, not far from Carnac, and the city of Jerusalem.

We set out this second network at a time between the fall of Atlantis and the coming of the Master Jesus, when we saw that there was a need for the Earth to hold and distribute that blueprint of Love which leads to a perfect balance in all the apparent dualities of life. The innate and universal tendency toward balance and order is represented for you in many different cultural traditions. You have long known the caduceus symbol with its two serpents representing the paired male and female qualities of wisdom—one active, the other passive—entwined around the central staff, or axis, of life. In the Hebrew Kabbalist's tree of life, it appears as the middle pillar of equilibrium, linking the manifestation of Earth with the Crown of divine creation, set between the twin pillars of positive expansion and negative contraction. In the Chinese tradition it is symbolized by the unity of yin and yang, the two poles of alternating and endless change, each containing the seed of the other.

The paired and curving bands of energy from Jupiter were recognized early in your history and marked in similar ways to the solar places of power. Human awareness of their male and female characters was shown in the siting and dedication of many temples, consecrated in Greece, for example, to Apollo or to Athena—the progeny of Jupiter in his earlier name of Zeus—and in Britain and France, churches dedicated to Michael or Mary, each located on the appropriate band of energy. As White Bull has said, "the Christ energy is not to be confined by geometry," and so we created them in a different form from the other nets, giving them sinuous curves to meander unpredictably over the globe, bringing the positive and negative energies together or apart wherever needed. Like the solar bands around which they twine, they contain a number of parallel impulses of energy, but with alternate polarity and flow.

When the Master Jesus walked the Earth, he manifested in physical form the balance of these two poles of energy in order to bring back into human life the possibility of a perfect unity between the male and female principles and between spirit and matter, and so recall you to higher levels of consciousness. You might see in this intention one of the meanings of the search for the Holy Grail in Arthurian legend.

Each of the other planets in your solar system projects onto Earth its own net or grid, of definite and regular pattern, which carries the particular characteristics of our archetypal influence to all the physical kingdoms of nature. Some of these eight regular grids have been dowsed and measured, and are known to your scientists—named after them, in fact—but their origin and purposes have not been generally understood since the early days when astronomical and astrological influence was recognized and integrated in life.

The smallest is the Hartmann Grid, which runs north-south and east-west, with a regular mesh pattern of quite small dimensions that tapers toward each Pole. It emanates from the Moon, the satellite planet that circles your own. The level of its energy is quite low, well below that of healthy humanity, being but a reflection of the Sun and lacking, in fact, our direct contribution.

The next in size you call the Curry Grid. It has a diagonal lattice structure and comes from the planet Neptune. Both these networks have alternate positive and negative lines, which at intervals are doubled as a larger grid, thus somewhat increasing their effect. These patterns are known to some of your doctors, who have found human illnesses, cancer for instance, associated with persons working or sleeping at the main negative intersections which can be located by dowsing. These are not, however, the cause of sickness in themselves. Rather, they act as focal points to which certain emotional states and negative influences can become attached; the planetary influence can amplify these and even trigger physical symptoms in those with a weak immune system. Symptoms or weaknesses are always present in the etheric level or aura before becoming physically manifest. In such cases it is possible for you to shift the lines of the grid mentally, or to move away the affected person physically. This, however, does not remove the underlying weakness in the person, who may attract negative energies in another location if there is a vulnerability in his or her own etheric field.

Then there are two larger north-south systems, the Peyres Grid emanating from the planet Pluto, and another, as yet unnamed, from Mercury. A diagonal lattice, the Wittmann, comes from Venus, and another of similar size emanates from Uranus. Saturn projects a north-south grid and a more widely spaced diagonal network, named after a Dr. Schneider, comes to you from Mars. All fluctuate with the phases of the relevant planets and are also affected by the cycles of the Sun.

In every case, except for the Moon, which is under a devic influence from Earth, there is an Archangel who typifies and projects a particular attribute by using the net of planetary energy. It was the Archangel Uriel who handed over to the devas the responsibility for the Moon. Uriel's function, as you may have read in the Book of Enoch the prophet, was to establish measure and dimension, to assist mankind with the precise marking out of the sacred sites as a reflection of the perceived movements of the heavenly bodies. While this is now a roving commission to apply cosmic principles when earthly energies reach high enough to accept them, Uriel may still be called upon to raise the energies of a locality where there has been a serious distortion of the natural order.

Planetary Origins

We remind you at this point that most of you, along with many of your predecessors, originally came from the planets and therefore retain close, if not conscious, links with them. Long ago, your ancestors brought new awareness to the indigenous peoples already living upon the Earth, who had evolved over many millennia from the basic animal form and condition. Humans never were apes or monkeys! There have been many different influxes of souls of celestial origin. Among them were some who came to remind those who had journeyed here earlier of the level of consciousness needed for working in full harmony with their new home, in the hope that they would not become lost in the material density of the Earth's vibrations.

All of you inherit certain talents and characteristics from your former homes in the heavens; some have been used wisely, and many unwisely, as you began to forget your inheritance of wisdom and its origin.

The study of the heavens, the motions of the planets and their influences, has had a long history in the world's cultures. Its inner significance, however, has been lost in myth—reduced to entertainment level—since it divided into two separate disciplines, the one extrovert and the other introvert, of astronomy and astrology. There is a real need for the unification of these two sciences to provide greater comprehension in the coming times, to enable you to understand yourselves and your place in the universe and permit you to take an informed and greater responsibility for the future of the planet.

There are remnants and obvious memories of your ancient links with the Sun, the Moon, and the five nearer planets in the familiar French and English names for the days of the week: as in Sunday; Monday or Lundi; Mardi, the day of Mars; Mercredi, or Mercury's day; Jeudi, Jove or Jupiter's day; Vendredi, the day of Venus; and Saturday, Saturn's day. You inherited these names from the Romans and from Greek astronomy, while the words Tuesday, Wednesday, Thursday, and Friday come from Norse and Teutonic gods with similar planetary associations to the Latin.

We would like to tell you about the influence which emanates from each Archangel, and reaches you through the solar system and its planetary grids, affecting each one of you through your own chakra system, whether you know it or not. We begin with the Sun, since it has the greatest power and a particular significance, being responsible for your time cycles and Earth's seasonal rhythms.

Archangel Michael and the Sun

Michael, which means "like unto God," occupies a central point, with the Sun itself, in the Archangelic world of light, serving as mediator with the lower worlds of manifest form. As the Archangel of truth and beauty, Michael is the exemplar of responsibility. He helps you to become responsible for yourself by finding your own inner strength and destiny, and enables you to pass through the shadows without despair by keeping the light of divine consciousness in your heart. Michael is sometimes represented as the weigher of souls, balancing those whose souls are full of light with those whose souls are in darkness. As leader of the Archangels in this present era, Michael at this time is creating a focus or direction for the fulfillment of the highest human potential and the balancing of all polarized energies, including male and female qualities.

We quote now part of a message channeled from the Tibetan Master Djwhal Khul: "The principal use of the Sun is electrical force adapted to the need of the great average majority, in all the kingdoms of nature. . . . electricity . . . produces the cohesion within all forms, and sustains all life during the cycle of manifested existence."

The incoming energy from the Sun, for which Archangel Michael is responsible, is in fact the full spectrum of the electromagnetic life force. For humans it is now absorbed through the upper four chakras of the body; in earlier times, when the chakra system was developing, it was taken in through the solar plexus area. In the case of Earth it enters at the sacred places we have spoken of, sometimes called light-centers. The life force of the Sun is the activating principle of DNA, which in turn holds the genetic blueprint of form in all living structures, including that of the Earth itself. This high-frequency force is held, stored as in a reservoir and replenished daily, in the solar net— the leyline system—which crisscrosses the globe.

Some of you will have seen the crop-circle symbols of recent years, impressed into the summer crops of Britain and other countries. They

THE STANDING STONES SPEAK

have several layers of functioning, among them to bring to you joy and humor, and to indicate our presence. Amongst their many varied patterns was the Kabbalistic tree of life, which is both a diagrammatic model of the universe and a representation of the Archangelic forces. Many picture the planets and are to remind you whence you came, but their principal purpose is to make injections of additional higher energy into Earth's fabric, an input to help release you from fear. You will find, therefore, that all of them are located upon energy bands, chiefly on the solar net and sometimes on one of the Jupiter bands, connecting directly into the distribution networks.

Until the destruction of ancient Atlantis, the Sun's vital rays were directly received by the planet Earth, as they still are in many respects by all life forms. After that time the principal connection with this source of primary energy was redirected to our chosen locations, ready for the next stage of human evolution, so as to provide focal points where the incoming vitality could be recognized and enhanced by human activity. Many thousands of years before the coming of the Master Jesus, therefore, we began to elaborate the network of light-centers for your future benefit, linking them up and ensuring that other living, unseen entities, guardians of the Earth spirit, would be available to look after them. Now we are reinforcing them in certain places with a new, parallel pattern bearing universal Love, making use of the energy of Sirius, which is for you the brightest star system in the heavens. Where this new field of Love runs alongside the existing solar bands, those of you with enough sensitivity will be able to identify it. We can call it the Eleventh Global Grid.

In fact, the whole solar system has an interplanetary pattern of vibratory fields or emanations in which each planet affects the others, in addition to their magnetic fields and the gravitational forces which control their orbits. At one time we established a solar network on Mars which still exists, but has been closed down as it is no longer needed; it was set up at a time in that planet's history when a form of life existed there which paralleled that on Earth. The Martians destroyed their atmosphere, and the continuation of life there beyond the stage to which it had evolved became impossible. Accordingly Mars was abandoned for the more favorable conditions on Earth, which at that time knew nothing of pollution. There are no solar nets on other planets since the life-forms there did not need them.

From early times the Sun, as the co-creator of life and source of light and warmth, was an object of worship for men and women. It was recognized as the origin of the appropriate alchemical and electrical conditions for the generation and continuance of physical life. The power of its energy field, which you can feel upon your body, is an indication of the power of the planets which may be felt only on a more subtle level, but is nevertheless a vital addition to the rays of the Sun.

The timely withdrawal of the Sun's energy as Earth rotates creates the round of day and night, and then, with the Moon, the seasonal pattern of the year. Its vibrations feed and strengthen the body, pulsing through its organs in a daily rhythm; it is present in all life, allowing it to bud, blossom, and decay in order to be constantly reborn. The

Sun is bountiful, all-embracing, the quickener of life, providing light, color, and all that is necessary for physical existence.

Archangel Zadkiel and Jupiter

Zadkiel holds the power of mercy, while the corresponding planet of Jupiter has a dynamic but ultimately balancing influence, particularly on the extremes of human behavior. Together they are thus responsible for the twin bands of Christ consciousness on Earth, which follow their separate sweeping courses but never fail, at important points on the globe, to come together and entwine in actual and symbolic harmony.

Zadkiel provides the stimulus to develop by testing human trust, providing situations in which faith in the workings of divine power is required. This puts you in a position where you have to take the bull by the horns by making a positive choice, trusting that you will find fulfillment in a new and unexpected direction. Zadkiel helps the creative forces to flow more easily, by balancing inspiration with your mental and physical activities.

It is from Jupiter that many of the beings of the devic realm have come, with the ability and commitment to temper and regulate the incoming energy at every sacred place as part of their service to the Creator.

The Moon

As the Earth's satellite, the Moon has enlivened the night with the Sun's reflected light, and fascinated humankind for many thousands of years,

THE ARCHANGELS AND THE PLANETS

in particular during the period of matriarchal domination on your planet. During a part of that time there was also oppression of the male, so that the expression of female power and womanly fertility was exaggerated by the exploitation of men, exemplified in Greek myth by the annual death of the king and his replacement by a younger successor. You may even see this now in colonies of bees, in which the male drones are excluded from the hive when their purpose of fertilizing the queen is complete. It was during the megalithic era in the Mediterranean lands that femininity and worship of the Moon goddess began to be suppressed, followed by the time of patriarchy from which you are only now starting to emerge. In human historical times the coin of exploitation was effectively reversed as male energy reclaimed its power and expressed it, in a similarly negative way, by the domination and oppression of women and the rejection of feminine intuition.

Now, as many of you are realizing, you are entering a new phase of history, one of equilibrium without that domination of gender, leading toward a perfect partnership with no struggle for power. On either side is a recognition of the positive aspects of self in which each person can become whole and unwounded in response to the other. Such relationships have been hard to achieve, although they once existed in what we might call conditions of sexual naïveté during the early history of the human race. Now they will be forged anew with the inner strength of Love and mutual awareness.

The Moon represents the balance of masculine and feminine qualities, which is why it has been sometimes perceived as male and sometimes as female. Because of its ability to create equilibrium, and its association with your emotions, the vibrations from the Moon can bring about a new unity in the human psyche, which will accept messages of wisdom from the subconscious and integrate them into a fully awakened state of being.

At different times the Moon has been the object of great veneration since the watery or fluid nature shared by Earth and humanity is subject to its gravitational pull as it waxes and wanes each month. You know that the Moon influences the tides of the sea, your daily emotions, and the menstrual cycles of women. It also affects the comings and goings of souls, both the birthing of a soul into a physical body and its return to the world of spirit on leaving the body.

In farming tradition, the phases of the Moon are important in the planting, germination, and harvesting of crops. There are appropriate times for the growth of all your vegetables and fruits because they are directly related to those cycles, and each species is linked to one of the planetary webs of energy. Crops that are grown or eaten out of season or place do not always retain the relevant planetary input, so that vitality and the intended nourishment are lacking. More specifically, you are beginning to realize from research that each species of tree and plant has an affinity and rhythmic connection with a particular planet. All oaks, for example, are physically influenced by the regular alignment of Mars, Earth, and the Moon. Beeches respond to a similar line-up with Saturn, and birch trees to that with Venus. Moreover, as some foresters and gardeners are aware, plants—trees in particular—

have a preferred direction in which to face when transplanted, as indeed have the standing stones, a sense of which Japanese gardeners have long been conscious.

As the Moon changes shape and position from your earthly viewpoint, it expands the solar time frame of day and night into a monthly rhythm which in turn makes up the thirteen equal months of your former lunar year (the year and a day of so many fairy tales), not quite in phase with the solar year of your somewhat inconvenient twelve-monthly calendars. The abandonment of the lunar year followed the move to a male-dominated society.

Being stronger at night and representing the subconscious mind, moon energies can put you in touch with your own subconscious through dreams, which often give essential insights—showing you, sometimes symbolically, sometimes factually, what has not been recognized in the awake state and may need to be thought about and changed. Issues that arise when the Moon is full often show you what is out of balance in your life. Its light can reveal unresolved pain. As it reflects the light of the Sun, so it also reflects what needs to be healed and what otherwise hides behind normality.

The Moon can help you to trust your feelings and find treasure and wisdom in darkness by filling your life with its quiet light. Its characteristic qualities play a large part in re-creating balance, being picked up mainly by the lower chakras of the body, which are in turn closely related to your emotions, then drawn up to the pituitary gland to affect the entire nervous system.

On the other hand, its level of vitality, as received in the global Hartmann Grid, under a devic influence, is less than your own, unlike all the other networks which have substantially higher light frequencies. For your better understanding of the subconscious, we have recently introduced a new grid of higher spiritual energy that exactly overlays, but does not replace, the Moon's projection and complements it. The bright light of Sirius, partner to Earth, enables us to do this and it is the Archangel Metatron who oversees this new process.

Now we wish to say more about the other planetary systems and our Archangelic governance of them, as a synthesis of the influences that reach Earth through the global grid patterns. We remind you, once again, that we are working in this way in order to serve the Creator, with the specific intention of raising the consciousness of humanity to higher levels; that this is beginning to happen will be evident to some of you.

Archangel Zaphkiel and Neptune

Zaphkiel, the Archangel of contemplation and understanding, with the distant planet of Neptune, brings in sustenance for the soul, making you more conscious of soul and so of the possibility of reconnection with divine unconditional Love. This role will in due time find its fulfillment in the balance of spirit and matter, in the human experience of receiving nourishment from the interlinked worlds of Earth and spirit.

Zaphkiel can help you find inspiration by making physical efforts, providing support to bring back dignity into your life. Valuing life, and finding ways of making your own contribution to it, will become more important, as will the ability to see a larger part of the picture than is possible from a single perspective. Sometimes, too, Zaphkiel and Neptune will help you to reach into your own depths of the mind and see what lies there. They will keep your feet firmly on the ground while you reach to the heavens for guidance.

Some of the elemental beings, the elves, came once from Neptune and have since returned there, now that their period of service on Earth has come to an end.

Archangel Raziel and Uranus

As Archangel of wisdom and revelation, Raziel uses the energy of Uranus to bring radical change into your life in the form of a new understanding. It will come through a connection with your inner teacher so that your life can be truly guided by the hidden wisdom of the Creator. This change may cause some upheaval. New attitudes will develop, bringing higher thoughts into your conscious mind; such as "How can we do this better than before, with more care for people's real needs?"

Raziel inspires by bringing in wisdom and the insight to see below the surface of things. This is an unblocking, freeing energy, a release from stagnation and a return to cosmic order. With Uranus, Raziel

121

encourages positive action, which does not mean taking the easiest route but certainly the most creative and unconventional one.

You will be reminded of unseen powers and your connection to them, recalling trust when there is doubt or fear. The forces of oppression, which place no value on life, will be overthrown by the power of Raziel and the revealed "secrets of God," or cosmic law.

Souls from Uranus are working among you at this moment, not incarnated but at an unseen level, opening your minds to change and helping you to heal old conflicts.

Archangel Metatron and Pluto

Metatron stands at the crown of the tree of life, in parallel to your chakra system, where the will of God enters to inspire each Archangel, and each person, energizing all creation with the dynamic attributes needed for a perfect world at each spiritual level. From this source of universal light spring all the powers of creativity manifested in material form by humanity.

The powerful flow of vibrations from Metatron and the most distant planet of Pluto is causing some disturbance in your lives now. You will be aware of this as you seek to establish harmony between the male and female energies in your lives and within yourselves, because your most intimate relationships will be affected by it. Metatron thus empowers transformation, the ability to change the old into the new, making a sacred space for the process of rebirth required by the upward pull of evolution, and changing anything which fails to resonate with the highest truth. This is why Metatron has taken charge of the new, uplifting energies now reaching Earth from Sirius.

There are souls from Pluto incarnating at this time upon your planet. It is their first incarnation and they have no past karma to resolve. They are sensitive, pure, and honest, and will freely speak their truth. Since these souls have a vast capacity for giving and sensing where Love is needed, they will be working to restore equilibrium, not for personal gain but for the common good. They are able to express the true meaning of the Christ consciousness by balancing the warmth of female nurturing and the strength of masculine compassion within each individual.

Archangel Raphael and Venus

Well known to you as the Archangel of healing, Raphael is linked with Venus. That planet, on which many of you have experienced a former existence, though not in a dense physical body, is like others in projecting a mediating influence into your world. This is to blend divine and personal love, bringing the one into the other to raise human relationships to a higher level; in other words, helping you to become truly human.

Through such loving relationships the forces of Raphael and Venus combine to open up areas of the unconscious to a new awareness. They have much to do with the healing of human emotions and the search for harmony in all aspects of life. Raphael may be called upon whenever help with personal healing or with creative projects is needed.

Raphael can bring all opposing forces into balance by allowing humanity to breathe in the inspiration of love and beauty and translate it into creative ideas and forms. The process will transcend sorrow, making a pathway for joy in its place.

Incarnate amongst you are a number of souls from Venus, making their contribution to this wonderful harmony of creative love and inspiration.

Archangel Hanael and Mars

Hanael upholds the state of Grace that has been lost and will be restored by the changes to come. Using the planet Mars, where many of you have had a former existence, this Archangel brings confrontational energies to the fore, and exposes them so that they cannot be ignored. This can be a painful process whenever you have failed to address an important issue.

Hanael and Mars thus challenge every situation that lacks the creative element and so does not produce any growth for the soul. Change can be effected by directly confronting the shadows and questioning your usual conditioned response to difficult circumstances. This combination of forces can be quite ruthless if you are heading in an inappropriate direction, but it can enable you to find inner strength in ways not previously experienced. Hanael will bring conditions that assist the transition from one stage to the next, although the process of change may not be comfortable.

Thus the physical warrior can be transformed into the spiritual warrior, since all conflict takes place in the spiritual realm before it manifests on a physical level. With Hanael's help, the physical warrior can find the spiritual strength to overcome negativity, first on the inner level, then outwardly.

Those of you who came from Mars are more familiar with confrontation than are your brothers and sisters from elsewhere. Your experiences there will have shown you that conflict can only be resolved permanently, and without creating karma, with spiritual guidance, and that the firm power of Mars derives directly from that of the Creator.

Hanael can ensure that all who possess this type of challenging energy will be able to use it now for a higher purpose.

Archangel Gabriel and Mercury

Gabriel, a familiar name to the Christians among you, is the Archangel of that spiritual knowledge which lies behind all forms of existence. This knowledge has the function of raising your consciousness to make you more receptive to God's will and so to the laws of the cosmos.

Using the planet Mercury, Gabriel acts as an ambassador between Creator and the created, preparing human minds and bringing in more understanding before great changes take place. Gabriel lays the foundation of higher ideals, infusing daily life with spiritual awareness, often by giving you signs or flashes of intuition. These signs are for those who are in the dark as much as for others already moving into the light, since the spiritual growth of the whole of humanity is Gabriel's particular concern.

The power of Gabriel and the planet Mercury can create a vanguard army of bearers of the truth. New motivation and understanding will enable them to clear away dead wood so that new growth can begin. Certain souls from Mercury who feel intensely the challenge of these times will then be able to initiate fresh projects for establishing future global harmony.

Archangel Samael and Saturn

As the adversary and Archangel of judgment, Samael's influence, borne on the power of the mighty Saturn, permits you to accept the limitations of earthly time and physical life while also giving you an understanding of the immortality of the soul. It is necessary to acknowledge your limited scale of time so that you can act appropriately at the right moments in life, but the recognition of the immortality of the soul is never to be forgotten.

Although time, your linear time, forms part of the restrictive framework of Earth, many of you will develop a new attitude toward it by learning to live more fully in the present. Samael helps you to pass from one stage to another, as at the death of the body, by seeing each as a part of the process of growth. He challenges your ability to follow inner guidance when old patterns of behavior hold you too tightly, and encourages you to take more enlightened actions by enhancing your perception

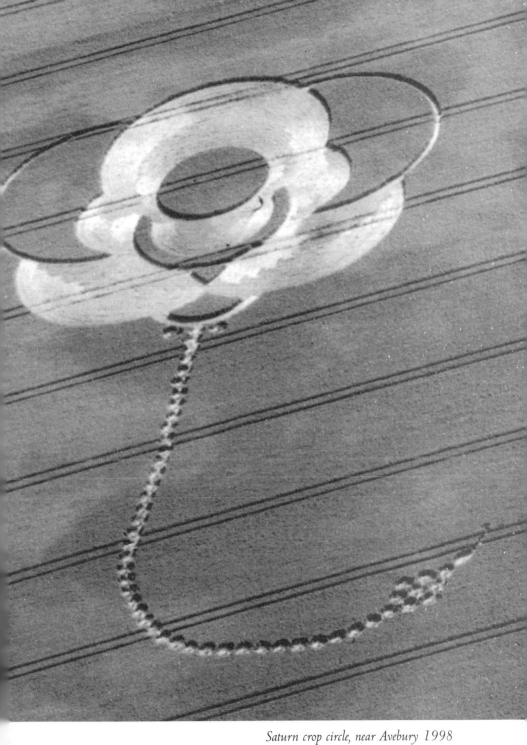

Saturn crop circle, near Avebury 1998

of the divine will. This is therefore a liberating influence that allows movement from restrictive, outgrown areas to a higher level of functioning.

The many souls from Saturn who now have physical bodies are working to release the restrictive, emotional patterns of the past which still oppose the natural flow of cosmic law.

Archangel Sandalphon and Earth

The archetype for humanity, Sandalphon is the guardian of your planet, standing upon Earth and reaching up to Metatron to share the inspiration of the divine light. Earth, being a receptor of the vibrations from the other planets, is the prime place where the influence from all the Archangels comes together as part of the universal flow of creative evolution. This combination of all our attributes is directed to the making of a physical environment, a Garden of Eden, which is intended to be preeminently suitable as the training ground for souls. It is a place of education in which the sensitivity of each soul can be developed through the fullest use of all the senses, providing the experience of love through an expansion of the heart chakra. Your planet is therefore a place of transition for your enjoyment and appreciation, but one that every soul, in furtherance of its own evolution, has to leave in due time. It is the distribution and availability of our archetypal qualities, by means of the planetary energies, which permit Earth to become such a special and sacred place for that process, able to reflect the orderly yet infinitely varied cosmos itself.

While on Earth you can manifest your visions creatively by endeavoring to work with both the material and the spiritual dimensions in all life's activities. This is a supremely important process and it is Sandalphon who has the task of holding spirit in matter for you. At the same time, Earth has the task and the means of providing your bodily nourishment from the wonderful abundance that was created for that especial purpose.

Humans were intended to develop the sixth sense of intuition and learn to trust it as a guide along the path of life. It is a bridge to the unseen worlds of angelic help above and devic cooperation below. Intuition can be your guide when rational information is limited or confusing, or when you feel too dependent on old attitudes and traditional beliefs that are not related to any inner knowing.

We want to make it clear to you that human beings are responsible not only for the planet, but also for their own relationship with the angelic realm from which the higher energies come. You have the joyful task of raising the vibrational energy of all lower realms, that is to say, the animal, vegetable, and mineral kingdoms, and not only by consuming them as food or making other uses of them. This obligation comes about because you have been given the ability to communicate and work with all other worlds, the devic, angelic, and divine realms. Human beings are the essential link, the bridge between these higher and lower levels on the ladder of evolution.

That was the plan by which planet Earth would receive cosmic intelligence and manifest it so as to raise the level of consciousness in the rest of the solar system. However, the present reality is very different. What we perceive in the energy field of Earth is much grief from unenlightened souls who are trapped between the astral plane and the Earth. Such grief is blocking the way, clogging the Earth's atmosphere and actually making it harder to raise the vibrations of energy. These souls, emotionally wounded, even distraught by repeated lives of trauma on the Earth, are unable to return to the Source. Similarly, they cannot reincarnate in a new physical body because the period for resolving karma is coming to an end. They have become trapped in a limbo state, without enough spiritual awareness to be open to receiving the help they desperately need to move on and continue their evolution.

More than anything, these trapped souls—some of them you know as ghosts—need human love, which many have never experienced. A vast input of human love and prayerful intention is required to release and raise them up so that the light of higher consciousness can truly enter and become visible to them. We, too, are working to clear the way but it cannot be done without human cooperation. You are the vibratory and self-conscious bridge between these different levels of existence. Yet you have developed such a fear of what you call the supernatural that you are fast becoming the weakest link in the chain. An awareness that will dispel that unreasoning fear is needed; supernatural is no more than an extension of what you classify as natural. The apparent barrier is due simply to your limited understanding and level of sensitivity, an overreliance on your physical eyesight, always looking out but rarely seeing below the surface.

We see that you have lost much of the faculty of wise discrimination through failing to fully develop your senses as was intended. This has restricted your capacity for inner knowledge and seriously weakens the link with the essence of creation. The faculties on which you are so dependent are, in fact, underused. In your mind you have already censored "the evidence of the senses." The evasionary tactics that you employ to avoid letting the light into your lives will have to be given up; they need to be replaced by a strategy of straightforward empathy with divine guidance. So much love and help is available to you if you only choose to reach out to it.

However, a change in your self-perception is beginning to occur. It is being made possible by the combination of our influence and the planetary energies, whose interlocking networks bind together the solar system and directly affect all life on Earth; this is what we are endeavoring to describe to you. An ever-increasing number of you are experiencing higher levels of psychic vibration due to the new infusions of spiritual energy which we are making available in the energetic networks, in the strengthening of the grids and by way of the crop-circle patterns. All these are boosting the long-established system, mainly to help the process of evolution, but partly to overcome pockets of negative energy.

Seeing yourselves in a new light will encourage all of you to take back your personal sovereignty, which means to reside within yourself, to be responsible, fully incarnate, and unwounded—to be human in the full recognition of your talents. You will see that your life *does* have purpose, that you *do* have a reason for being incarnate at this time, and that your contribution is in no way to be regarded as insignificant.

The discouragement you have all experienced in previous incarnations, and perhaps in this one too, has been insidious, challenging all inspired creativity and love. Now it will be less strongly felt; in fact you may see it as an illusion which can be outfaced and positively transformed.

Each of you is part of a larger plan, and you are returning now to the pattern of your own true blueprint. As we have said (and many of you will know), this will be painful if you resist your destiny. For a time there may be discomfort and unease as the new track runs alongside the old; but your soul has a plan for you, of which your conscious mind is as yet unaware.

There will be a rebirth. The phoenix will arise from the ashes of the past with a new strength and beauty. The old inhumanity, the selfish ego of the past, will disintegrate and allow a new and positive humanity to arise with greater understanding than before. In the fullness of time our original intentions for the fulfillment of human potential will become manifest to you all.

A Gateway in the Woods

Le Petit Ménec is the smallest of the Carnac alignments, overgrown and hidden in thick woodland, hard to find because it is not visible from the roadside. By the same token, though, it is the most romantic of all, with dappled sunlight falling on the stones, amidst the trees and yellow-flowering gorse—an ideal place, not much visited, for a quiet picnic and a bottle of wine. Some eighty stones remain, smaller and closer together than those at Le Ménec itself. In the early nineteenth century hundreds of them were removed and shipped out to build the lighthouse at sea on Belle-Île.

Hamilton and I followed the winding path between the surviving rows. In one narrow place the trail passes between two of the taller upright stones and at that point I experienced a strong tug at my body at waist level, pulling me back like an elastic cord. Startled, I repeated the exercise; it happened again, and each time with the same elastic pull. We sat down and did some dowsing, which revealed that what we had found was a portal, a gateway to other realms of being, perhaps parallel to our own, and it was still in use. Maybe it seems hard to credit, but I was feeling the pull back to another dimension and another planet . . . to Venus, in this case. We lacked the know-how to use the portal, fortunately—or we might not have been able to return.

It was time to reflect and question, so in a meditative mood we ate our picnic, seated on a fallen tree. Our Indian spirit guide had spoken earlier about portals and we had become aware that a few remain in England. Now the stones revealed that this was an important gateway for beings with souls similar to our own, but without our physical bodies.

We sensed, surprisingly, that there were no nature spirits in this sacred place; they had apparently left when the site became neglected. Ten devas, as guardians, remain. Assigned to such a place, it is not so easy for them to leave, but the nature spirits lose heart easily and can move away. At some point in time it will be necessary to invite them back and so restore full spiritual harmony to this beautiful part of the French countryside.

There are two other portals in the alignments. One is inside the place of assembly, the cromlech, at the western end of Le Ménec, where the hamlet is built inside the curved ring of the remaining close-set stones. Years ago one of the barns was converted to a crêperie, now closed. It was the favorite haunt of Professor Alexander Thom, the Scotsman who, with his son, Archie, spent many seasons surveying and making exact plans of all the megalithic sites. Mistrusting the local food, he used to bring Scots porridge with him until he discovered how good the pancakes were—he called them the "creeps." We were happy to think that insubstantial beings from other worlds, arriving at the portal in the barn, might feel the need to queue up for an earthly pancake after their journey.

—Natasha

CHAPTER 6

The Elemental Realm

Lord, what fools these mortals be!

—William Shakespeare

There are many beings who inhabit your planet with you but exist in other dimensions than your own. Since they have a different vibratory rate they cannot usually be seen by human eyes, although the inner spiritual eye may perceive their presence. They are souls who have maintained their bodies of light and so have little or no material density. Thus they have never become enmeshed in matter as have humans, yet they are tied to it by certain responsibilities for the natural world and by a necessary link with human beings.

We can call these souls the elementals. They are a part of the universal evolutionary process, but they can only move forward and eventually return to the Source through an association with humans. Their progress and spiritual nourishment are totally dependent on this. As it

Alignment at Le Petit Ménec

has long been denied them, they no longer feel a connection with the Source and have forgotten their origins, yet continue to serve. Although prophets and teachers have appeared for humanity throughout your history, there have been none for these invisible spirits of nature, whose function is to give support to mineral, animal, and plant life, and by that means enable human life to continue as part of the whole.

Until quite recently, these elemental spirits were presided over by other beings, the devic order of elves. But the elves, too, had lost their links with the divine, and had to find individual human beings whose own connection was strong enough to help them. As their period of service on Earth came to an end, they needed to find a source of higher vibrations in order to move on. The elves were troubled about leaving the nature spirits and their companions, the devas, to continue to work without them, and deeply saddened by the lack of human understanding. But with human help they were able to leave the Earth and continue on their evolutionary path. Some went to the planet Jupiter, others to Neptune. Their intention is to return to Earth at a later time with extended abilities for working with nature in a different way. You can consider them as being on a training course in another sphere of development. Elves, you may like to know, are beings of light taller than humans; they are not as in your picture-book illustrations, although there are other beings similar to those images.

All the elemental beings have made a choice to be in service to the planet and to provide the conditions needed by those other souls, your own, who have metamorphosed into human form. They have dedicated themselves to the various tasks of maintaining the environment which humans have been neglecting. Their original understanding was that this would be a cooperative effort.

They can be helped to remember their divine origins by your acknowledgment of their presence and in the celebration with them of the seasonal cycles, especially on the solstice days when certain places upon the earth are empowered with a regenerative input of vitality. Like humans, the elementals have become separated from the Creator, but unlike you they have never lost their sense of purpose. They can be freed from their isolation when humans reach a certain level of spiritual awareness, one that corresponds to the elemental presence. This will uplift them and transform their present state to one of gladness.

When you left the Garden, the former human acceptance of the angelic and devic realms was lost; you denied the help and guidance we have to offer and began to feel alone, almost out of our reach. Some of you have fallen, in life's preoccupations, from the human level to that of the animal or vegetable realm, thus being unable to fulfill your inherited assignment to raise those kingdoms to a higher state. In this reduced condition, human beings can themselves be raised up only by some event dramatic enough to shock them out of complacency and into a search for a deeper meaning in life. They have to reach through and surpass the lower levels before even attaining the fully human state in which it is possible to make contact with the angels.

Every one of you has a number of spirit guides who are willing to work with you. Your own guides will be attracted to you by your specific activities and talents; if you are a composer of music, then you will be inspired by the spirits of celestial composers to interpret cosmic melodies. Spirit helpers can also be those whom you knew in other lifetimes, or even ancestors. They are empowered by your conscious awareness of their presence, which of course also empowers you. Our own help in the past has been limited because we have not been able to impose on your freedom to make choices. This restriction is coming to an end as we intervene on the Creator's behalf to save humanity from its own shadows. In the process of bringing in the light, we may even override some of the choices made from your subconscious mind if they do not agree with your soul plan.

Now and in the times ahead, many of you will be renewing your links with unseen helpers from above and below. You will need to distinguish true light from false, remembering that, as Victor Hugo said, "in the deepest shadow there is latent light." If you happen to be living at the vegetable level, the light of the animal level will seem very bright and you might be satisfied with it. Many become identified with one level only, not realizing that there are others. You have to realize that the ladder of existence has many levels if you aim to ascend it and speak with the angels; and Jacob's ladder has had many beings climbing up and down it other than the angels themselves.

Elementals, however, are aware of the necessary functions of the different levels of being, and they know that it is only the truly conscious human who can supply the balancing factor for a harmonious interrelationship between them all.

Efforts to find a spiritual connection in your present Western culture have too often been only on the mental plane. Fearful of the old pagan deities and mysteries, you have become apprehensive of direct personal contact with the world of spirit and the natural energies of the Earth, preferring, as some of you do now, a world of virtual reality to actuality.

Many of you have an impoverished or fearful understanding about the other beings who share your environment. There is much for you to understand about these other beings in order to release that fear and become open to communication with them. Trees, for instance, are beings of great importance to planet Earth, though sadly not always recognized as such. They are sources of old wisdom, and, as we have said, are directly linked with the movements of particular planets. When life was at an earlier, experimental stage and many prototypes were being tried out to see which would be the most adaptable, trees were able to take up their roots and move. They were splendid, powerful beings and could travel where they would. The soul beings which have now taken root as trees have given themselves to be your shelter in the woodlands. Besides being a source of usable material and purifiers of the air, trees are guardians of wildlife and keepers of the ancient ways in that they hold the key to many ailments through their medicinal properties. They work with the nature spirits in the transformation and balancing of the energies in the atmosphere and the maintenance of life in the soil. They have memory, and those who know how can ask them questions and receive answers.

As part of the great tree of life, we, as Archangels, are totally in service between the Creator and creation. We are not in evolution as you understand it, but oversee that process on your planet. As individual souls we are whole and undivided, not separated into male and female as you have been, and you may call upon each of us by name when the occasion demands. It is truly important that you call us as witness to any enterprise or gathering of people, whether for work or celebration. If you do not invoke our presence and so create a blessing on your activities, you leave a void which can then be filled by the influence of the dark forces. These forces have no need to be called in, for they are always present in the background, whether invited or not.

From the angelic world, the greatest gift for humanity is discernment—the innate ability to distinguish the truth—so that you can make choices from a point of illumination instead of from the shadows. We bring also the recognition of your origins in the skies. When what we offer you is comprehended with clarity, and wisely made use of, you will find that life becomes an expression of the highest human qualities; you will be working with the inspiration of the stars, uplifting and transforming the energies of the Earth. Working with angels provides the alchemy for change to a far higher level than is possible when you rely upon your own limited human resources. Ultimately you will become more self-reliant by raising yourselves to a higher level of consciousness.

Past attitudes have prevented you from understanding that angelic help can always be called upon by the individual. So often we have been regarded as unreal, or if real, then unapproachable. We remind you that we are here for each one of you. Historical lack of trust in anything higher than human authority has resulted in your responding to difficult situations with fear, and without the ability to bring in higher energies. With our assistance and your own clear intention, you can bring illumination to your troubles and more easily resolve them. We know that many of you are tired of coping with problems on your own. The past patterns of adversity will be changed as we help each of you to bring light and Love into your lives. The angelic host, long accepted as the messengers of God, works as a group and is not differentiated into individual beings, nor by gender. If it is appropriate for you to invoke the angelic host when you need help, their multitude will be present in an instant, just as any one of us can be.

Once all angelic and devic beings were known as the Shining Ones, and that is the meaning of "El," which forms part of our naming. That is how all of us were perceived when the veils of your perception were less dense and more easily penetrated by vision; but the characteristics and allotted purposes are very different for each order of being.

It is the devas and the nature spirits who occupy the sacred places on Earth, the power points of solar or Jupiter energy, and sometimes angels are also present when there is work to be done. All have their clearly defined functions. Devas handle and protect the incoming energy, which enters as a kind of raw material and has to be converted for use, woven into many strands and vibratory patterns of the life force in order to suit every form of created life. They can close down a site if it is misused, or reduce the energy there according to the sensitivity or insensitivity of any human beings present. You might call them spiritual technicians, guardians of the power supply from the Sun. Some devas act also as guardians of place, the *genius loci*, with the ability to manifest in visible form, perhaps as an owl or fox or whatever might be appropriate at the time, in order to make their presence known within the frequency range of human vision.

The spirits of nature share the sacred places with the devas and are more numerous. They are responsible for the well-being, fertility, and life cycles of all flora and fauna, ensuring that the life-giving energy is held in the seed of plants, and in the young of animals of every kind. They maintain the balance and vitality of water, air, and earth, even against increasing pollution by humanity. Through their presence and commitment, both land and sea will eventually come to cleanse themselves.

Unlike the devas and the angelic world, these nature spirits exist as separate male and female entities, but work together in small communities of group consciousness. They were known and respected in many of your earlier cultures, being for the Greeks the nymphs, the naiads, the dryads, and the oreads. In a similar way, for the Aboriginals and the Native Americans, they are the spirits of water, trees, and rock, as they were in the animistic lore of your Celtic predecessors in Europe. These souls hold the blueprint of all natural forms.

Female nature spirits look after plant life, birds, fish, and the elements of water and fire, while male spirits are concerned with trees, animals, insects and reptiles, microorganisms, and the elements of earth and air. If support is given by way of human acknowledgment of their activities, their work will flourish; but if not, these spirits, like human children, become discouraged and lose vitality. It is possible to sense their presence much as diviners can detect water and know its volume and purity. Occasionally a nature spirit will travel with a human from one site to another, seeking to experience something of human spiritual life or needing to work in another place, as they are essentially nomadic and free to move from place to place. They enjoy human company but only at an uplifting or creative level.

Because they are outside the cycle of life and death as you know it, these beings are not part of the process of soul reincarnation which humans go through. They can live for many hundreds of years and at death are absorbed back into the consciousness of their group. There are people who at one time were spirits of nature and then chose to have a life in human form, bringing with them their love of the natural world.

There are also entities we can call gnomes or goblins. They are the masculine spirits of the North, the deep earth, and the mineral kingdom. At each sacred site you will find a single goblin whose function is to anchor the light energies beamed at your planet from the Sun. It is the rock and mineral energies that make this possible at each place, and that is why crystals and minerals contain so much light and color. The goblin, being responsible for the slower pulse of life in the mineral kingdom of Earth, works in a frequency range lower than that of humankind, but can occasionally be seen if he chooses to appear.

Although associated with them, he cannot see the other elemental spirits of a higher frequency and so often feels that he is working alone. Quite often a goblin will become misplaced when roads or buildings are constructed in his territory, or if he loses touch with the devas, as sometimes happens. If he becomes disturbed, his call for help can cause problems for people. (Any misplaced etheric life-form that seeks to draw attention to its predicament can have a similar effect.) A misplaced goblin will want only to be returned to his rightful place, and this may be effected by any person of sufficient sensitivity by asking for help from a higher source. Because the disturbance has usually been caused by human agency, it needs to be corrected by human awareness together with angelic assistance.

Building work of any kind that is undertaken without an appropriate ceremony is liable to cause problems. In Eastern countries such as Indonesia this is well recognized, and a ritual is performed to inform the spirits of the earth and ask for their cooperation. In Iceland, too, the presence of earth spirits is acknowledged and great efforts are made not to disturb their abodes. Some of them will object to a lack of consideration and, if deprived of their appointed place, can become mischievous, even causing accidents, in order to draw attention to themselves. They are not malevolent, but are actually asking for help, which can be given by asking that they be returned to their rightful place.

It was once the custom for country folk to put out a bowl of milk or gruel for the "little people" and this was a relic of past respect and communication, now lost. It will take more than a bowl of porridge to ensure real cooperation with the beings of the elemental realm. Their relegation to children's storybooks has trivialized your understanding of these beings and their functions, but shows that somewhere they still exist in your minds as a memory from the past. If you can imagine something, then on some level it exists, and if you can then remove your fear of the unknown, you are on your way to a greater empathy with all that is.

At some of these special places of antiquity, those of you who are open to the presence of spirit may find that alongside the groups of elementals are the spirits of early indigenous men or women. These souls evolved on the planet with the help of the nature spirits. Earth is their home and they are greatly disturbed by what is happening to it. But for the present, they are unable to move on; their sensitivity to the true nature of the planet makes it impossible for them to reincarnate amongst you. They will continue in evolution only when a sufficient number of humans have attained a high enough level of consciousness to raise them up also and enable them to extend their experience to dimensions beyond this planet.

The gatekeepers are small groups of devas who activate the portals for out-of-body journeying. Many of these secret portals are still in use, available to incomers of light from other galaxies and planets who are entering to help with the transitions to come. These souls do not remain at the gateways but travel immediately to where they intend to work for you, unseen, and in most cases, benevolent.

Awareness of the essential contribution of these and other invisible beings is of the greatest importance at this period of your history, when materialism threatens to swamp the human spirit. They have much to teach you about their work with the creative forces of the universe and the vital energies of the natural ecosystem in which you live and of which you are such an important part.

When the Creator expanded and breathed out, inspiring life in all created forms, each being was fully identified with its Maker despite the myriad species, realms, and characteristics. As groups or as individuals, they recognized their function and place in the spiritual evolution of the universe. Of all those countless beings, none have so far separated themselves from the Creator as have humans, even denying their origins. By misusing their priceless gift of choice, they have lost themselves in the shadows.

From our point of view it seems that humans have become desensitized, some through an overabundance of material possessions, others through a lack of them, disregarding in both instances their fundamental need for spiritual growth and connection. In either case, you have forgotten that the world was made rich and beautiful for you as a microcosm of the divine intention in all things. We remind you that each individual is an essential part of that cosmic order. Your spirit and your body are specially attuned, in the frequency range of your brain and organs, to the Earth, so that you each share basic characteristics that exist nowhere else.

In a parallel way, the elementals—from goblins, nature spirits, and the devas, right up to our own angelic realm—have electromagnetic

147

form and levels of consciousness that can be linked with those of humans. At the lower levels, in fact, they are dependent upon the quality of human consciousness to the extent that their work with fire, air, water, and earth and all the living forms of matter is directly affected by humanity's attitudes. So we can say that often you get the weather you deserve! The elementals carry on their work all over the planet and so are constantly around you; you could not breathe or even exist here without their subtle energies that enliven and balance all created earthly life. It is an aspect of co-creativity, in which their activities in the natural world coincide with our own, but not always with yours.

With the arrogance that has developed in humanity you have assumed that you were alone here, masters of all you survey. You have let slip the bonds that hold you to all things, seen and unseen, and attempted, in isolation, to impose your will upon the natural order. In due time this situation will be reversed, as you gain an understanding of your place in the universal plan and respect for the role of the unseen forces. In forgetting your connection with the higher levels of spiritual sustenance you have deprived the lower worlds of theirs also, for in this they are so very dependent on you. When humans are not able to keep a balance of the elements within themselves, the external expression of those forces can be very destructive, as you have seen in earthquakes, tidal waves, hurricanes, and fire storms. Human behavior can actually attract such elemental conditions.

Everyday life offers the possibility of conscious co-creativity with the elementals, with angels, and ultimately with the Creator. This is our shared inheritance. Such beautiful cooperation, consciously aligned to the Creator, has never been fully manifest upon the Earth, however; often the combination of forces has served only to activate the darkness, because humanity is wounded and constantly under the influence of negative emotions. The human race has not yet realized its potential for experiencing Love.

Releasing your great capabilities in the context of Love and cooperation will bring about a new world order, free from pain and struggle, and founded upon divine inspiration. By gaining an understanding of the function of the other realms of creation, you will be helping to restore the inner light in yourselves.

Chambered mound at Kercado

CHAPTER 7

The Masters

The rainbow raised up with me,
through the middle of broad fields,
the rainbow returned with me,
to where my house is visible,
the rainbow returned to me.

—Navajo poem

You have never been alone, help has always been there. Over the centuries a number of spiritual masters have come to you from their origins in the stars, because even from that distant perspective, they could perceive quite clearly what was happening on Earth. They knew they had to reactivate your light bodies, your auric rainbows, so they incarnated upon the Earth and lived amongst you to demonstrate the qualities of a "whole" human being. Their purpose was to remind you of cosmic law, to be seen to follow divine will themselves, and to act in accordance with the highest principles of Love, compassion, and wisdom. All of these masters have brought in various rays of the rainbow to provide illumination for the human race.

All that is needed for humankind to recognize its own divine origin is the acknowledgment that every soul is an expression of the Source, and that this expression can be diverse. Every human being can become a mystic, able to feel united with the Source of life and to use that connection for daily guidance. It is through the unique qualities of each person that the Creator can manifest the inspiration of the universe.

As an inspired soul, the Master Jesus took personal responsibility for bringing the energies of the Christ consciousness into the world. He was not contaminated by the Fall, for the shadow which had fallen across the human race had not darkened his soul. He taught that in daily life you can be open to the miraculous through the transcendent power of Love, by taking an attitude that does not judge but accepts the flow and changes of physical existence. He said that the human soul will eventually return whole and rejoicing to its Creator. By the example of taking total responsibility for his words and actions, he demonstrated the possibility of restoring humankind's inner balance with the divine.

He came to you from the brightness of Sirius, not simply with peace, but with the power of Love which creates peace. For you he distinguished truth from falsehood. This master brought radiance and the joy of a simple life, with the message that for every individual there is a destiny which cannot be governed or limited by material considerations when they conflict with divine law. His intention was to make clear to you the need to take personal responsibility for yourself and your actions, and not to follow blindly the dictates of society or religion.

The Master Jesus was born into a family that had an understanding of spiritual laws as part of the Essene community. The Essene sect was not totally acceptable to the occupying Romans, but was tolerated as long as Roman laws were not infringed upon. In an effort to live a peaceful life, members had to make many compromises. The Creator and cosmic law, the supremacy of the spirit, however, cannot be compromised indefinitely, for ultimately personal integrity suffers. The Master Jesus never surrendered his integrity. If the rabbis who knew who Jesus was—and some did—had accepted him and revealed the truth to their followers, the course of human history would have been changed.

Compromise simply means noncommitment to the truth, an avoidance of personal responsibility. There is no strength or fulfillment in compromise, only an illusion of flexibility that leads to resentment and dissatisfaction on other levels, because the underlying issues have not been addressed. Fanaticism, on the other hand, is the reverse of compromise; both are the work of the darker forces. There is a great insecurity about those who range between compromise and fanaticism, compromising others and sometimes themselves with rules and prohibitions; both are weapons of control. Fanatics seek control through confrontation while those who prefer compromise seek power by more devious means. Love and joy are totally lacking in both these postures. When Love seems to be present, it is actually conditional, and so is an illusion. Never allow anyone to compromise your personal integrity with the temptation of his or her half-truths. Remember that the purpose of your soul's journey is to develop your own integrity, to purify your inner self so that it resonates with the light and purity of gold and becomes untarnishable, incorruptible. Fanaticism and compromise are a denial of the natural flow of life and the perfection of cosmic truth. Fear is at the root of both.

We are speaking mainly of the Master Jesus because so many of you have been affected by the various doctrines and conflicts of Christianity, in which fanatics' distortions of his teaching have done much to delay the progress of the soul, instead of aiding it. His incarnation among the Jewish people was to remind them of their soul purpose, or covenant, that they should unite and share their special talents with all the races of humankind. Each race, originally deriving from the Creator, also has an actual planetary place of origin, a distinct soul purpose and particular talents to contribute to the development of life on Earth. For example, the Chinese peoples have in the past developed an understanding of the manifestation of the planetary forces upon the Earth, which is expressed through *feng shui*—the art of placement—by locating and working with the energies in the landscape. Chinese medicine works similarly in treating the body, by assisting the energy flows with acupuncture. The Jewish people have also an innate understanding of the presence of spirit in matter, traditionally expressed in a different way. Their ability to bring joy of spirit into the material world through their celebrated creativity was intended to be shared with others in order to enrich the whole.

If the potential talents and gifts of each race are not expressed positively and shared with wisdom, that same energy will turn inward and become exclusive, even unwholesome. It is so with entire races and with the individual.

The coming of the Christ was an opportunity for humankind to raise itself up, to escape from the shadows of closed minds, but it was an opportunity lost. We may say that it was not the divine intention for Jesus to be crucified; it was a possible outcome, and sharing in the optimism of the Creator, we had hoped it would be otherwise. The Crucifixion was a dark event for humanity, equivalent to the actual darkness that enveloped most of the planet after Atlantis fell. It provoked an era of denial and suffering. To persecute or to be persecuted is no way to experience spiritual wholeness or to live a balanced life. The Christ consciousness, which lies beyond all religions, is an essential ingredient for human life and the evolution of the soul which could have been accepted two thousand years ago.

The message of Jesus was soon suppressed and distorted as those in authority used the Christian religion for their own political ends. The arrogance of wealth and the tribal divisions among people were perpetuated, which might not have occurred if the wisdom of the Jewish mystical tradition had been combined with the enlightenment of Jesus Christ's message. He sowed the seed but it failed to germinate, even in his own land.

The Christian dogma which developed later under Roman patronage could never speak the truth, because it came from the desire for control. Indeed, the Church itself was structured upon the imperial pattern of power and authority.

There has always been misunderstanding, not only of Jesus' teachings but also of his death. Knowing the importance of his words for the human race, he demonstrated, by the sacrifice of his life, what was being done to the truth and what people were doing to each other in the name of truth. His death showed what those in authority—in this case the Jewish elders—would do to maintain their position, how afraid they were of the truth and its effect on their people. It was a warning that went unheeded and opened the way for countless more acts of brutality in his name.

The higher purpose that the Crucifixion served was that Jesus was able to maintain love for the human race, despite experiencing its darker inner state which he had come to lighten. His suffering was transformed into divine Love, freeing him from karma, and making it possible for others to reach through their pain into the light. He became the symbol for life everlasting after death of the body. You have not been given enough clarity in religious explanations about what this actually means, especially as the Church chose at an early stage to reject the truth of reincarnation. As a result, many orthodox Christians are taken by surprise at death; for when you die you are still the same person as you were in life, only without the use of a body. It is consciousness that you then have to work with, and if that consciousness remains fearful, still rooted in material values and unresolved problems, you can become stuck in the only experiences you remember. You cannot take yourself any higher, being unaware that higher worlds exist. Enlightenment does not come automatically when you pass through the veil. We see Christian graveyards full of the ghosts of those who do not even know that they are dead and cannot comprehend that they have moved into another dimension of a different potential. Their limited perceptions have prevented them from encompassing the light and moving willingly into it.

Life is everlasting. It cannot be otherwise; like all matter, it simply changes from one form of energy to another. The life everlasting which Christ held out to you is that which is achieved when the cycles of earthly karma have been completed, because only then is there freedom of spirit. He hoped to liberate you from this repetition, telling parables of truth which speak through your heart to your soul. The raising of consciousness in the comprehension of his teachings by those who heard them at the time would have meant an end to the accumulation of karmic obligations and your continuous entrapment on the Earth. Unfortunately, then as now, there were few who could see the deeper layers of meaning in the parables.

The work of Christ incorporated the energies of the sacral chakra, bringing the divine life force down into the physical plane and aligning it with the heart chakra, through which Love can flow. His apparent death on the cross was symbolic of the suffering humanity has to undergo when it rejects the spiritual truth. It did not have to happen, but it was chosen for him by the people of that time because they were not ready to accept his teaching. They preferred a life of compromise in the relative security of the status quo, whereas those who preached the truth of the message feared for their lives. Even the disciples of the time, with the exception of John, did not fully comprehend the significance of the Master Jesus. When the master reappeared to the disciples after the Crucifixion, it was to comfort them and encourage them to carry on his work. Their grief called forth his spirit to show them that physical death is not an end, but a transition.

In karmic terms very little has changed since those events, and the suffering has continued. The second coming, so often spoken of, refers to the emergence in your own hearts of the Christ consciousness—it cannot happen anywhere else. You will then have the power to overcome the pain and turn the darkness of the spirit into light.

Have you not thought it strange that the image of Jesus presented in your churches is that of the Christ crucified, suffering, powerless? That is how they have preferred to keep him, on the cross and under control. Few portrayals are seen of a radiant figure who has transcended negativity, which is the true message for you.

The real followers of the message of Christ are not those who set up a dogmatic system of worship, but those who develop an inner knowing from their own personal communion with the Creator. Humankind cannot live a balanced life and find fulfillment and personal integrity without in some way experiencing this individual receiving from the Source of all life. Attunement with the Creator will bring the guiding light of spirit into every part of your life; you can then become your own teacher without needing the props of organized religion.

The Patriarch Moses, who incarnated long before Jesus, lived also in a time of much discord, especially among the tribes of his region, when there was little integrity except among small groups of spiritually aware people. The Essenes were one of these groups, and there were certainly others who kept the faith with the Creator elsewhere, as, for instance, in India and China. Moses could see that his people needed guidance to make their lives healthier and more spiritually constructive. He asked for divine help and was given a vision of the true cosmic law by the Archangel Zaphkiel. Realizing that his people were not ready to accept this, and that he himself was not capable of changing their understanding, he surrendered these higher laws and asked for teachings more suited to those who had lost touch with their inner wisdom.

Then Moses received a second vision, whereupon he announced a set of basic rules for living, in the hope that they would ultimately lead people to accept the higher teachings. This second teaching, the Ten Commandments, was intended to align the solar plexus and the throat chakra in complete integrity of expression. But the Mosaic law, as it became known, was honored only in the breach and fell victim to misinterpretation, because the inner nature of humankind failed to develop beyond the expression of the lower emotions. People at that level are always the prey of those who wish for control.

When we saw that even these teachings were not heeded, it was decided in the heavens that the Christ would incarnate amongst the Jewish people, but with teachings available to all, not only to small, esoteric groups or to the initiates of secret, mystical knowledge. Sadly, the human state had still not evolved sufficiently to accept his message and many of you are still living with an interpretation of the old Mosaic teaching based on patriarchal leadership, unable to rise any higher toward the Christ consciousness.

Six hundred years after Christ, the prophet Muhammad—peace and blessings be upon him—working through the vehicles of the crown and the throat chakras, aimed to bring spiritual unity to his people. He laid the foundations of an autocratic rule, tempered by an unquestioning acceptance of the divine will. Rejected at first, he lived to lead and unite his followers and become the founder of the Muslim Faith. His teachings, recorded in the Koran as received from the Archangel Gabriel, were intended to foster compassion and the Love of the all-merciful Allah. Muhammad maintained the positive masculine principle, and as Moses had done, he set out guidance for daily life. Like those of other masters, however, his teachings have become sub- ject to distortion and misunderstanding over the years. Nonetheless, the extensive Arab conquests led to a period of great learning, which included tolerance for other faiths, notably that of the Jews. In truth, humanity needs to achieve concord with all other cultures, between man and woman, one country and another. You need to balance the demands of heaven and earth within yourselves, by making the fullest use of the human chakra qualities, the significance of which each master has in turn represented and brought onto the Earth.

The inconvenient truth of every message has either been ignored or become ossified in religious dogma. Judaism, the Muslim Faith, and Christianity have been, and still are, misinterpreted and misused for political ends, convenient labels for the domination and mental control of other people. Religious fanaticism, intolerance, and cruelty have long been the mark of the Christian era, and now are seen again in both Israel and the Muslim world, yet unlikely as it may seem at the present time, these perverse activities signal the forthcoming end of the rigid attitudes of your organized religious structures.

Some centuries before the coming of Christ, the Master Confucius left his heavenly abode to incarnate in China. Combining all the ancient teachings of that vast land, he gave his students a practical message of love that would unite society through discipline and wisdom. Affirming the male principles of traditional ethics, he taught that positive action in the world could come about only through education and knowledge. By activating the brow, or third-eye chakra, he created a channel for the divinatory wisdom of the universe in his contribution to the I Ching, the Book of Changes. Life can never be static, but it can, and should be, orderly. In darkness there is light and in light, darkness; in all things the opposing force is ever present to create the appropriate dynamic for change in life, which like a river always flows onward. That flow of life is taken in with the breath, courses throughout the body in the blood, and can then be manifested in actions that are motivated by wisdom and obedience to custom. A stable society was the Confucian aim, and this led to the establishment of China's mandarin class, educated and effective administrators whose system lasted for more than two thousand years.

Lao-tzu, at much the same time, brought a message that was complementary to the philosophy of Confucius. He preferred to stress the need for intuition, the feminine side of human nature. His followers taught the mystical way of being at one with the flow of the universe, through good actions that are not contrived but are instead a form of spontaneous attunement. In this, his contribution represented the alignment of the three lower chakras—the base, the sacral, and the solar plexus—making it possible to move higher and raise the human level of perception. As with Confucius, an acceptance of the natural laws of rhythmic and dynamic change was fundamental to his teaching, but Lao-tzu believed in the individual, the setting of personal example, rather than acceptance of the conventions of society. Like all the great masters, the concept of adherence to an intellectual dogma or fixed system of belief was anathema to him, since its result is a static, unevolved consciousness. From these ideas began the tradition of Taoism, the way of experiencing harmony through intuition and meditation, of attaining immortality through personal purification. Everything that is manifest comes from the great unmanifest void, the Tao, to which it will eventually return through the successive cycles of life, forever expanding and contracting. This movement between extremes is symbolized in the twin polarities of yin and yang, set within the circle of the universe.

In India, during that same period of spiritual advance, the Gautama Buddha began his teaching of humanity's way to develop beyond the repeated incarnations upon the wheel of life. He taught that enlightenment can be attained by nonattachment, by shedding the illusions that arise in human life in which there is no perception of what is real and what is not. The laws of impermanence and constant change were an essential part of his teaching; resistance to the flow of life, attachment to fixed ideas, to the concept of self as an identity separate from the universe, are all futile and caused by ignorance. The round of human suffering, of karma, can be brought to an end, however, by gaining insight and practicing right seeing, right knowing, and right actions. To that end we can say that he was working to integrate the base chakra energy with the integrity of the solar plexus. His course is the middle way; the practice of contemplation, compassion for all living things, the surrender of personal will and desires, in order to reach the bliss of total liberation that comes from being at one with the universe.

Other masters have worked with different parts of the light-body for you, bringing in different rays of light and color, reminding you to find your own inner light, and helping you to become the prophesied Rainbow Warriors. We want to emphasize, however, that those we have so briefly mentioned were working, between them, with all of your principal chakras. It can truly be said that all the spiritual teaching needed by humankind has been given to you.

Many masters and inspired messengers have come and gone in your history, providing guidance for those who have lost their way. Feelings of love, compassion, and humor have identified them and always distinguished them from false prophets, of whom we have to say there have been many as well. True masters never lose their connection with the Creator, nor do they have human karma to resolve. Moreover, they do not come into the world to found religions. Their purpose is to demonstrate the freedom and essential divinity of the incarnated spirit in humankind.

Religions and dogma divide people; spiritual truth will unite them. You see that the messages of the masters have all been the same, varying in approach and emphasis according to the time and place in which they were given. Together they have worked to illuminate the human mind and activate your light-bodies. There was no conflict in their teachings until they became distorted by lack of understanding and regulated by human institutions under the influence of the dark with the intention that you should remain separated, fearful, and thus be controllable.

Over the past two thousand years, which you in the West know as the Christian era, no place on the planet has been able to enjoy harmony. At no time has humanity managed to achieve a sustained period of peaceful living in balance with cosmic law. Even the two hundred years of the so-called Pax Romana was a period of military control that led to eventual collapse. The Arab conquest and the Venetian, Spanish, and Turkish empires were established by force for the acquisition of wealth. The British empire and, now, American world dominance—both trade and technology-based—have been backed by military power. In Asia and the East, Chinese and Indian cultures developed early to an advanced level but were repeatedly destroyed and renewed in successive struggles for power and huge migrations of people. Despite these parallel periods of continual strife and movement, there remain fundamental differences between East and West, although we see that the end results are very similar.

The philosophies which have long been developed in the East place an emphasis on mysticism—the life of the spirit—with material wealth as a secondary consideration. As a result, many are prepared to accept their lot as poor and homeless, and only a few hold political power and wealth. We can say that in Africa the situation is similar but in a less conscious, more tribal way. In the West, where rationality and theology make an uneasy blend, the situation is reversed, with the emphasis upon material success and little recognition of the needs, or even the existence, of the spirit. While many are still poor and some homeless, the majority have a high material standard of life; and some with great commercial power are able to acquire immense—and super-fluous—wealth, unmatched by any spiritual awareness.

Everywhere there have been such distortions in your attitudes toward spirit and matter, yet they form a whole, they are one. So our message must be still to consciously unite spirit with matter, integrating these two elements in your thoughts, words, and actions, for it is the only means by which balance can be attained, and human life on Earth enabled to continue.

India is an example of a land of great spiritual awareness, where there is now not just a separation, but a conflict between spirit and the material. The spiritual beliefs long developed there have led to denial of the importance of the material, and of the physical body. There are those who now wish to develop the power of the material forces without the spiritual essence, and others who wish to preserve ancient spiritual attitudes and ignore material needs. If India can ever achieve a harmony between spiritual wisdom and physical existence, then it can become a truly great nation, but if it cannot there will be continuous and widespread strife.

Much of India is truly magnificent. Its people remember the creation myths and the old gods who symbolize the manifold qualities of the "One." The sacred places are recognized as homes to spirit energy. One of these, a very special place in western India, near Nandurbar, is a light-center, a source of energy central to the importance of that whole continent, where an exceptional concentration of cosmic forces enter and are radiated outward. One function of this place is to enable individuals to maintain their link with other cosmic levels. There have been many mystics and teachers who have lived in India for that purpose, encouraging the way of enlightenment—the necessary link with higher worlds—by their ascetic manner of life; the Master Jesus himself spent time there. This center of energy will shift eventually to a place in the Western world, as the peoples of the Western nations regain their spiritual balance.

It is no longer necessary, however, to go to a particular holy place to receive inner guidance. That is now possible wherever you are because the cosmic energy that enters through the power points of the planet is now becoming more manifestly radiant than ever before. Equally we can say that although the age of the manifest teacher is almost past, and you are learning to become your own teachers, souls are being prepared in the spirit dimensions who will be able to give their guidance only through the medium of channeling, inward receiving. Among these voices will be those of the indigenous peoples of the distant past, the Aboriginals, whose identification with their landscape and all living things can show you what you need to know about working with the spirit of the Earth. These souls will not be returning to Earth, as they have moved to a higher level of being and no longer require further experience of life in a physical body. Their understanding of the integration of spirit and matter will now reach you increasingly through the channeling of your contemporaries.

Between the two principal world philosophies or attitudes we have described, there lies another way of life in which that earlier resonance with natural law has not been totally corrupted or polarized. We speak of the few remaining people who still live in the wilder and more remote parts of your planet, for instance the Kogi Indians of Colombia, the Bushmen of southern Africa, and the last of the traditional nomadic Aboriginals of Australia. Many of these survivors of the past are leaving your planet and taking their wisdom with them. It will not then be accessible except through channeling.

We simply say that it is desirable that you cultivate an outlook that expresses the potential nobility of the human race and a lively respect for the power of natural forces. These simple qualities have been lost through an inadequate, unbalanced system of education, which has failed both to honor individuality and to point out the essential symbiotic relationship between the environment and all aspects of human life. It is not surprising that so many young people have lost respect for their teachers.

The human race has long been stumbling in the dark, guided only by the dimmest of torches since the bright lights were extinguished; the going has been rough, judgmental, and full of fear. The gleam of the torch has shown up so many others who reflect only your own pain and separation from the Source, and over many years your struggles have continued in that semidarkness. You have been motivated by anger, resentment, and fear, living with a recurring pattern of negative emotions from which all the masters have sought to raise you. You have turned against your fellow humans instead of seeing that the real foe is the fear in your own hearts. Instead of opposing the negative forces within your own hearts, you have externalized them and attracted hostility.

Few understand the implications of the masters' messages: that if you can cooperate with the powers of the universe your strength will be immense, because you are respecting the natural order of creation, as the early mystics and shamans did. The powers we speak of are neutral, but they exist and can equally be used for dark or light purposes. Misuse of them is at great cost to you and the planet. Some of your leaders who have worked with these powerful forces during times of war learned to manipulate them for their own ends, but in the long run such negative use caused them as much darkness as they inflicted on others. But there have always been those who worked, and still do, in the light of cosmic truth, in ways which will restore the inner light of the spirit in your heart, and who can show humanity how to live for the highest good of all.

At certain times in your history it was thought important that a balance be kept between those who spent their time praying for others and living a religious life, and those who lived in the secular world and pursued material activities for themselves. In fact, this equilibrium could not happen, since in each sphere was corruption and little spirituality. We then found it necessary to establish places in remote and unsullied parts of the planet where a truer spirituality could be practiced by those who honored the highest truths. This continues today, but that balance between spirit and matter is inherent in each of you and you are responsible for finding it in your lives now.

There are today, and always have been since civilization began, those who live on the edge of society. There are many individuals who live by begging in the midst of wealthy societies. These people are also teachers. While their behavior seems to be an embarrassment in the West, in the East it is considered an honor to give alms to a beggar, considered as a holy man, who then confers a blessing. This is a way of avoiding responsibility, actually, on both sides. It seems to free the giver from praying for guidance in his own life, although he acknowledges that some form of prayer is necessary, and it also appears to free the holy man of responsibility in the material world. Now, we ask you, is the beggar more or less holy than the one giving the alms, since neither has the balance right? In the eyes of the Creator all creation is holy and to be revered as such. Are those in the West who beg less holy than those in the East? Or any less part of the Source?

The behavior of so many who beg is alarming to you in the West, for these are not holy men, nor are they praying for you. What are they doing? Rejected by the society in which you all live, standing outside it yet reaching inside it for help, could they be there to teach you something? Perhaps they are saying, "Society doesn't care. If it did, we wouldn't be here." Perhaps they are saying that within your community they have not had the care, support, or nourishment they really need, and so cannot find their own strength to survive in it. You call them failures, but where is the failure? It is within the society that rejects and abandons its own members.

Some of those who beg on the streets have unconsciously chosen to do so to help humankind, to jog your memory. Their way of life is the crystallization of an emotion which reflects a part of society as it now feels, that is to say, helpless and powerless to effect a change. Many feel that they have to turn their backs on any hope of a supportive environment, and there is a lesson here for all of you. How much longer will your own environment continue to support you? Your religious, educational, political, and medical institutions have made you dependent, but they are failing you while you are losing your personal power to them. The more people there are living on the streets, the more faults are apparent in the structure of your society.

These souls are a mirror to the current process of disintegration. They suffer on your behalf as a warning, as do many more in the slums and the shantytowns of certain parts of the world. Some beg for their daily bread, others scrounge and steal. "But there has always been an element of this," we hear you say. Yes, but only since there has been fear in people's hearts. What in comparison are your own inner and outer resources? Upon what are you dependent? If you lost everything you value, where would you look for strength and support? Can you feel love for these people, or do they frighten you? Maybe you can sense that they are all part of a greater truth and that they are showing you the present distortions of life.

We have heard you say that conflict is a necessary stimulant to progress in life. It is true that the dynamics of conflict encourage you to move on, but it is rapidly becoming a misuse of divine energy for you to be forever in conflict, and has given rise to the situation in which you believe you have to compete to survive. This is a negative and destructive form of thought. A better way of using energy has to be found. There are those who wish for the opposite of conflict, in peace, but this too has its problems, for in your idea of peace there can be stagnation and no opportunity for growth; whereas life is eternal flow and change. There is another way. When your personal energies are no longer focused on and drained by negative issues, they can be available for true creativity, which is expansive, stimulating, and empowering in that you are able to work once more with cosmic principles, this time for the highest evolutionary good.

You may be able to visualize a world in which everyone is loved and cared for, whether they fit into your present conception of society or not, and we suggest that you do this. You may then foresee a time and place where every incarnated soul is nurtured and encouraged to develop his or her own particular highest creative potential. This is the awareness needed. This must be the goal of the education of your children, who need to be loved and to be inspired by creativity.

All of you can now become your own spiritual masters.

CHAPTER 8

The Rainbow

When the Earth is sick
and the animals have disappeared,
there will come a tribe of peoples from all cultures
who believe in deeds not words
who will restore the Earth to its former beauty.
This tribe will be called
Warriors of the Rainbow.

—Native American prophecy

W e have said that your light-body, or aura, is all that remains of your original form. The physical body you now have is simply a denser form of light with a lower frequency range. Linking it with the aura are the chakras, each one related to an aspect of the physical body and responding to a different color.

These chakras or gateways are the invisible, energetic links between the endocrine system of the body, its internal organs, and the ethereal external energies. The chakras, having higher rates of vibration than the body, surround and influence it. They have long been recognized in Eastern cultures as specific energy centers in the treatment of ailments. Europeans too are now becoming more aware of the importance of these centers and their use in healing. Ancient peoples knew that the patterns of the cosmos are repeated in the design and functioning of the human body, a principle not alien to contemporary quantum physics. Each part and major organ is under the influence of the cycles of the different planets.

There are seven principal chakras and a large number of minor ones, mostly connected to the limbs, and all of them have fields that extend beyond the physical structure of the body. The main gateways are the crown at the top of the head; the third eye, or brow; the throat; the heart; the solar plexus; the sacral, or spleen; and the base chakra, which is at the root of the spine.

In a general way the three lower chakras relate to your physical characteristics and the three upper ones to more spiritual aspects, while the heart may be regarded as the intended intermediary between them, a meeting point where spiritual energy is brought down, and earthly energy drawn up.

To reestablish the necessary rapport between humanity, the Earth, and the solar system, there will be changes in the human chakra system, leading each one to vibrate with its appropriate rainbow color. This will happen through your own healing process, which will also allow new energy points to open up between the principal seven. In particular, the heart chakra will expand to encompass a greater love for all life. Remember that life includes those mineral and other forms which appear to be inanimate, as well as what for you is obviously alive—the trees, birds, plants, and animals. All these are expressions of other soul forces which, like your own, are in evolution and service, each one being an aspect or fragment of the single universal Soul of the Creator.

An etheric chakra beneath your feet will open to reconnect you with the Earth. You may be out walking one day, barefoot upon the ground perhaps, when it happens. You will feel the power of Earth beneath your feet, and the strength of your connection with this enormous being, which like you has a soul energy and thus a spiritual commitment to the Creator to evolve. The Earth, too, has a chakra system, and there are many places where the ground actually resonates with the input of cosmic power, which can be experienced as healing and uplifting energy. Perhaps you are familiar with Kahlil Gibran's words: "And forget not that the earth delights to feel your bare feet and the winds long to play with your hair."

Humans are not simply creatures who walk about on the Earth's surface doing what they will; they are the intended link between the consciousness of the planet and that of the universe. You matter—*you are matter*—and how you behave has an effect on other matter which may be felt beyond the Earth itself.

Those of you who are attuned to spiritual development through such practices as yoga have consciously learned to draw in cosmic nourishment through your crown chakra, but it is not always remembered that this energy is also entering the Earth around you, and needs to be transformed by human beings—the link—before it returns to the cosmos. There is a danger in simply bringing energy down, since it cannot remain static—it is always in movement. You can use it

Cromlech at Le Ménec

positively only when it is anchored to something in yourself. It is only by being grounded—through the celebration of life in your relationships and your work, in the creative expression of your talents, and by your involvement in the welfare of the planet—that can you make effective use of these higher energies.

By consciously connecting with them at the places of power, drawing energy up from the ground through your feet, and then drawing higher energy down through the crown chakra in a two-way flow, you will be actively intensifying the earth forces and recharging your connection with the divine. You can become empowered, and the Earth will be revitalized in a form of shared communion. By doing this you can actually change the rate of vibration in the area and of course, increase your own.

Therefore, it is essential for human beings to recognize that this is an involuntary process. It takes place wherever you are, but becomes more efficient when it is consciously done together with an acknowledgment of your responsibility and ability to act as transformers of all these flows of energy. It is an absolutely unavoidable process. The currents of energy can be seen as the embrace of cosmic and earthly power, enhanced by the human link, by which you are actually helping, not only yourselves, but also other levels of being to evolve. This is part of what it means to be in service to the Creator, working with the flow of life and recognizing the importance of its unified nature.

The etheric chakras open and close in response to internal and external stimuli, as impulses increase or decrease. Each chakra, having a relationship with a major internal organ, resonates at the same frequency as the corresponding organ, while the polarity of the major seven chakras is alternately positive and negative from one to the next. As your healers know by the color and activity that is sensed or seen with the inner eye, they indicate the state of inner health of both body and spirit.

Thus, long before a physical symptom is noticed, it is present in the auric field, since the spiritual malaise always occurs first. If not recognized and dealt with, in due course it will manifest its counterpart in the body structure. As the parts of the physical body receive both cosmic and local energies through the chakras, so each organ processes or holds a different emotion or feeling. Illness results from a distortion of the true pattern, which gives rise to a blockage of energy or weakness of function that finally becomes an obvious symptom. It is this level of perception that is so lacking in Western medicine; true healing cannot take place unless the disharmony in the aura and the spirit is dealt with first. There may be a remedy for the symptom, but if the "dis-ease" or discomfort is still within the person's energy field, then the problem will reappear in the body. It is therefore of the utmost importance to include emotional and spiritual healing along with the appropriate physical treatment. When both emotions and spirit are healed, the physical symptoms will often disappear because there is no longer anything to support them.

Healing is essential on all levels. That is what will open the chakras to light and make the human rainbow shine.

179

THE STANDING STONES SPEAK

The Seven Chakras

The base, or root, chakra was actually the third to develop in human evolution, after the fall of Atlantis, when the body had attained a greater physical density. Your bodies are the physical manifestation of the four traditional elements. The base chakra is connected to the elements of earth, which represents the physical world, and of fire, which represents the spirit. The reproductive organs and glands are related to the base chakra, which in its full potential is seen as red, taking in energy that grounds and roots you, and giving a sense of being connected with Earth and at home in your body. It contains the feelings of sexual love and tribal or community well-being. Out of balance, however, this chakra energy causes sexual disturbance, feelings of separateness, and sometimes an anti-community attitude of aggressiveness. Many people who commit antisocial actions have disturbed base chakra energy. Much love in early childhood and an instilled sense of belonging can prevent these situations. Properly flowing, the base chakra works with the heart chakra to ensure emotional balance in your life.

The sacral chakra is related to the elements of earth and water and so to your human emotions. It is orange in color, connected to the adrenal glands, kidneys, spleen, and the small intestine. It was the second chakra to develop, enabling you to feel a sense of community. It also supports the reverse feeling, enabling your development of an individuality which is recognized and appreciated by others. The latter feeling is an adjunct to the function of the adrenals, which prepare the body for resistance or a hasty retreat in the face of danger. Judgment, rejection, or feelings of shame or unworthiness will affect you through this energy center, inhibiting self-esteem and the ability to function positively within society. Some tribal communities, for example the Native Americans, were happy to recognize that each member of the community had a unique gift to bring to the group—as indeed is possible today. But usually there is little recognition of the gifts each of you has to offer, and few individuals value their gifts enough to develop them.

Being formed from the elements of fire, earth, and water, the solar plexus chakra is the meeting place for spirit, physicality, and the emotions. This chakra is linked with the physical organs of the gallbladder, spleen, liver, and pancreas. It was the first chakra to develop in humans. The solar energies gather here to be utilized by the body, and are later developed to maintain your individuality and personal integrity within society, without becoming enveloped by the group consciousness. Its energy color is a protective yellow, helping you to be your true self in the face of external confusion. If it is in balance with your other chakras you will not feel confused but centered. Any discordance with the external world disturbs the solar plexus, and most personal problems become locked there until they are healed. There can be both absorption and loss of energy at this point. When in balance, this chakra enables you to see difficulties as opportunities for growth; out of balance, you are more likely to be reactive in behavior, unable to find your own truth or to be sufficiently discriminating in your choices.

The heart is the middle chakra, and was the fifth to take form. It is connected with the elements of air and metal, and to the thymus gland, the lungs, and the circulation of the blood. Its color, green, is the symbol of growth and of the transforming power of the Christ consciousness. The innate wisdom of the heart has the ability to transform all other energies in the body, both emotionally and physically, and when it is functioning well, that is what happens. Situations that are surrounded by negativity can be changed from this point of energy and positive solutions found. If a person speaks from the wisdom of his or her heart, then good decisions will be made. When they are so full of fear and hurt that choices from a place of pain are made instead, there will be a malfunction and the heart energy will be blocked. When a person is unfulfilled, then the heart feels sadness, and the spirit is low because the lungs are not being filled with vitality. All other chakras are affected and inhibited, because the heart is the most important organ in the body.

The fourth to be formed, the throat chakra, has evolved to give you self-expression, individual eloquence rather than a merely tribal means of communication. It is the true blue of inspiration and its highest qualities of expression, being connected with the thyroid gland, the vocal cords, and the larynx. Linked to the elements of air and metal, the etheric realm, and the mental energy of thought, it is the holding tank for the creative intelligence of the other chakras. When it is in balance, you will be in command of a situation and be able to say what you feel about it, truthfully and without any investment in the outcome. When out of balance you will have difficulty in speaking your true feelings, for fear of an outcome that you may not be able to control. You therefore develop a tendency to internalize things that are not expressed, whether your feelings or your creativity, which in turn causes a restriction in the throat area, possible difficulties with speech or breathing, and eventually problems with the rest of the body.

The brow, or third-eye chakra, is connected with the pineal gland, and to a lesser extent with the pituitary, controlling hormone levels and the processes of your growth. On a physical level the pineal is the light receptor for the body. Light entering through the eyes is processed there, enabling the body to respond to seasonal and environmental changes, to become one with the natural harmonies. On an etheric level the pineal receives the light of cosmic intelligence and wisdom. The sixth chakra to develop, it is through this center that your sixth sense, that of intuition, works, helping you become aware of the expansion made possible by higher guidance. This enables you to attain a state of inner knowing that will help you to become aware of the environmental energies at work in the world. When in balance, this chakra shows a beautiful indigo color. Out of balance, you can easily become controlled by others, because you do not trust or cannot draw upon your own inner resources. Life then does not fulfill your expectations.

You can observe from history, particularly in your well-named Dark Ages, how the intellect has stifled the life of the spirit by the suppression of intuition and the denial of feminine wisdom. That lack of balance effectively prevented you from feeling part of the "wholeness" of life. Consciously or unconsciously, control was taken by people of authority in the name of religion and logic—the light was excluded. Today your brow chakra is even further from its normal functioning due to a quite different factor, the universal use of artificial lighting, which has deprived you of the daily rhythm of the natural light cycle.

The crown chakra was the last to develop because it can function fully only when all the others are active. Linked to the pituitary gland with the element of fire, it acts as the gateway for your higher consciousness. Before the skull hardens in the human baby, light enters directly through the crown chakra to encourage bonding with the new environment while maintaining the soul connection with spirit. When this chakra is not fully developed in the adult, spiritual energies cannot be utilized appropriately. Ideally it was intended that you would develop the positive potential of each chakra, and be fully grounded in the earthly energies before the higher, spiritual energies enter through the crown. This was the requirement for all the initiates of the early mystery schools. We hardly need say that this does not always happen at the present time. The crown chakra is violet, and when fully balanced you are connected to that higher truth of your soul destiny which enables you to meet life's challenges in a positive way, using inner guidance and all the qualities of the other chakras. If this chakra is out of balance with the others, you will lack the ability to overcome difficulties and find it hard to make decisions. You will constantly seek advice from others, and be completely thrown by certain life situations or any input of stronger energy; possibly becoming mentally unstable in the process. That is why there is a danger in opening this chakra before the others are well developed; it can be very damaging, as the incoming energies will not find an outlet to contain and process their higher frequencies.

The human being is potentially a sacred rainbow, one who has the possibility of working with and through all the colors of the auric rainbow, gaining earthly experience in order to attain the full spiritual clarity of the visible light spectrum. The harmonics of colors were well known to the Atlanteans, the Egyptians, and later the Greeks, who had an understanding of the healing properties and the corresponding sounds of the rainbow colors. Pythagoras developed a system of musical medicine, finding that certain harmonies could produce a healing process. This ancient practice, currently being investigated, will prove to be of great benefit for the future. Some of your musicians have been able to see the colors of the harmonies with which they were composing, just as some artists can interpret sound into color. Color has its counterpart in sound and shape, as alternative versions of the same frequency.

All our archetypal attributes, symbolized for you in the Kabbalist's tree of life, can reach you in the vibrations of light within your chakra system. This is the way in which humanity is open to receive the messages of divine inspiration we speak of, by direct assimilation of the planetary influences.

When the human rainbow is fully developed you will be walking with the angels; your own light will connect with that of the Creator. The Master Jesus could not have performed miracles if his light-body or chakra system had been out of balance.

The angels surrendered their personal will to the divine will long ago, but the surrender of human will to the divine, not yet realized, will put you in direct touch with your own higher purpose. One of the tasks in human life is to learn to distinguish between the ego-based personal will and the true will of the Creator. This is possible only when all judgmental attitudes and the fear surrounding them are released. Then you will begin to have the confidence of knowing that you are a part of an infinitely larger pattern within which your personal destiny lies.

By working with the etheric chakras and their related emotions and with your physical and intuitive senses, the appropriate changes will come about so that you can eventually become the prophesied Rainbow Warriors. All the teachings of the masters have been leading to this glorious event, the restoration of your light-bodies to their full brilliance. The rainbow in the sky is a reminder of this. It is a bridge that links the earth with the cosmos, reminding you where you came from and how you will return there. Becoming the human rainbow in all its clarity is the only way back to the light of the Creator. The rainbow bridge is always there, even when obscured by the clouds, and when you see one there is always a little feeling of joy in your heart as you are reminded of the magic of the universe.

What prevents the human aura from shining out is that it is so often muddied by negative thought-forms and clouded by a lack of emotional clarity. The personal rainbow that surrounds you is your sensory shield, allowing information to be filtered and to pass both ways. When the aura is clear, your intuition will be heightened; when it is cloudy, the incoming information will be unclear and you will have difficulty discerning the truth.

Breathing energizes the chakras. Learning to breathe light and color into your chakras, perhaps with the addition of sound or toning, will clear the debris of the past from your bodies. Practice breathing in the appropriate color for each chakra, and then breathe out the old fears. This takes time and patience, and the more difficult you find it, the greater the need for it.

The act of breathing is not taken very seriously in the Western world. It is considered merely a necessary automatic process, a guide as to whether or not life is present. However, it is much more than this. Some of the mystics of the East, yogis and others, discovered many of the secrets of breath. Years of discipline enabled their bodies to transcend death, remaining conscious and passing through it into their etheric bodies. The physical body then dematerializes and the etheric body becomes visible; this can be consciously achieved over a period of about three days after the "death" of the physical body. This has enabled some adepts to live for hundreds of years with the same body, bypassing the process of reincarnation before returning to the Source. The Master Jesus used this method to enable him to continue his work after the Crucifixion.

You are aware that breathing affects your metabolism. It also affects your level of consciousness and can create altered states of consciousness. Controlled breathing can be used to activate the chakras and balance them. Usually, controlled ways of breathing are used only to cope with certain life situations such as childbirth, or to ease difficult states such as panic or shock. If you are frightened, you will breathe in more fear through quicker, shallow breathing.

Regular deep breathing, on the other hand, is a way of inhaling nourishment by bringing in more of the life force. Deep exhalation is a way of returning the gift of life to the planet, to the plant kingdom that absorbs and transforms what you cannot use in a process that maintains the earth and its atmosphere. In this manner you and life's other forms exist in an essential cycle of symbiotic relationship.

Inhaling is motivated by your conscious mind, for it is the will to live and activate the body. The outbreath is the subconscious mind releasing that which it does not need. This outbreath massages the fourth chakra, the heart, preparing it for a new intake of air. It is the holding of the breath between inhalation and exhalation that enables you to gain access to the higher levels of your soul consciousness, making a space to allow them in.

Breathing is an instrument of alchemy for the creation of change. Specific, controlled ways of breathing help to focus the mind to direct your actions. Breathing brings into balance all the elements within the human body, enabling the aura to shimmer with light as the rainbow of perfection. It is a means of carrying spirit into matter.

Signals

Sometimes those who have experienced psychic disturbances of various kinds in their homes ask Hamilton and I to visit. On one such occasion we went to a house in the Devon countryside. It has been converted from old farm buildings, and after a talk with the couple in residence we made our usual check for the energies in each room. Rather to our surprise, we could not find a single energy line or reaction to our dowsing there. The owners then told us that they had previously called in another dowser who had, as he thought, dealt with the problem by drawing a protective circle around the house to free it from any external negative influences. However, this had not stopped the peculiar disturbances about which the owners were now very concerned.

Further dowsing detected the presence of several ghosts, unseen but attached to the house. We all sat down to talk about the problem. It emerged that all these ghosts were relatives of the owner. They had died young, without really fulfilling their ambitions; rather, they had passed their whole lives doing what was expected of them by others. The owner, a middle-aged man, said he had been part of an extensive family in which everyone had always been too busy working to spend any time with one another. Now that most of them were dead, he deeply regretted his own neglect.

The owner felt, in fact, that he had reached a turning point in his life. He and his wife were living in a large house that neither of them liked very much and there seemed to be no good reason to stay there. He had reached an age at which he could retire and travel the world as he had always wanted, yet he still felt a strong commitment to his work and his colleagues.

What I received then was that the spirits of his relatives were very concerned that he should not follow in their pattern. The reason for their causing the disturbances was to make clear how important it was that he should follow his heart and live his life more fully, retire early, and travel as he wished.

We continued to talk, but tears were streaming down his face—his sense of duty to others was so strong that he did not feel he was allowed to fulfill his own wishes. Then, quite suddenly, the lights in the house started to flash on and off repeatedly. As the large chandelier continued to pulsate in regular fashion, first the television, then the VCR, turned themselves on and off. Concerned, the owner's wife switched off the chandelier, but it made no difference. She turned on two small table lights which promptly joined in the party. Even when she turned everything off at the switches, the electrical system went on flickering without pause in the kitchen. It was clear to me that angels were in the room, though no one else could see their own special light, a signal of their presence. The energy I felt was so very intense that I knew the relatives of this man had so much love for him, and he had such remorse for ignoring them, that they were determined he should get the message. He was to sell the house and retire, letting others take over, and free himself from the commitments and ties he no longer needed.

Everything gradually calmed down, and the flashing stopped when we felt that the message had been accepted and understood. Although Hamilton and I never learned the outcome, we hoped he had the courage to follow his heart and rejuvenate his family tree. If he didn't, the ghosts are probably still there.

—Natasha

Alignment at Kerzerho

CHAPTER 9

Empowering the New Jerusalem

*Mystical experience is necessary to understand the deepest nature
of things, and science is essential for modern life. What we need,
therefore, is not a synthesis but a dynamic interplay between mystical intuition and scientific analysis.*

— Fritjof Capra

Planet Earth is a powerhouse fueled by the elements, that is, the
mineral realm and the force fields of the cosmos. It is possible for the
human race to make use of these resources in ways that do not poison
the planet or upset its inherent system of balance. Within the Earth
there resides a store of potential energy, much of which has lain forgotten and unused since the disappearance of earlier civilizations.

The material worlds of minerals and crystals, for example, contain
energies that do not pollute or contaminate. They are waiting for a time
when the human race can recover its integrity and learn how to tap
these sources of power, safely and for the benefit of all. The nuclear
energy you have begun to use is a part of this and not necessarily
inappropriate. It is a little premature, however, since its development

took place in the context of war and can therefore be somewhat pernicious, being tainted with negativity.

During the destruction of Atlantis many of the crystal caves slipped into the bowels of the Earth, to be removed from human access until a more evolved stage of your development had been reached. Meanwhile, you have discovered the fields of electricity and many ways of generating and using them. This form of energy, too, is capable of abuse, not least because you do not yet fully understand it. You live in an electrical universe. Electricity is not a modern invention or discovery, it has always been there as the binding element in what you know as matter.

On the one hand, like all energy in the universe, electricity is neutral but can be misused by humanity or malicious entities. On the other hand, it is sometimes a useful link between us in the spirit realm and you in the physical realm because we share that force and can send you simple signals with it. When your house lights flicker, it is not always a fault in the system, it may be an otherworldly means of attracting your attention!

In the play of cosmic forces upon them, the rows of standing stones at Carnac and many megalithic structures elsewhere generate local energy akin to low-frequency electrical fields through an interaction with the quartz and mica particles in the structure of granite. The Carnac groupings were made from this particular crystalline rock, not simply because it was available but because it could hold the energy input from the Sun. The whole area of Carnac is alive in an electrical sense; it is an excellent "plugging-in spot," a good place for recharging your own spiritual and physical batteries. It is truly a place where our spirit input meets with the energy potential of matter.

We chose that site because the power generated within the stones has enabled our messages to be encoded there. The positive and negative energy fields to which we are referring do not represent good or bad in your terms. One is the active and the other the receptive qualities inherent in all life, the movements of the pendulum seeking equilibrium. Each stone, and at Carnac each row of stones, carries a polarity that is alternate with its neighbor; they are bound together in an alternating current.

As a form of life, quartz and crystals work very closely with the heart chakra. When they are programmed with clear intention they can receive, transmit, and amplify vibrations of various kinds. For instance, they can use the wave form of light to send love or healing to a person or place. They can be used to send light to areas of darkness or unrest and, more simply, to tune in to other electromagnetic signals such as radio waves; thus they have a capacity to hold information, and may be used for communication.

Remember, however, that human beings need to come to a certain level of ability in self-empowerment to avoid losing their own power to that of the crystal kingdom. This kingdom exists to serve as a tool and has no desire to control humans, but needs to be respected and used with care. Even without its aid your mental powers of higher intention can achieve similar results.

Because crystal carries within it the rainbow prism of light, the clear truth of the Creator on Earth can reside within it. It has the ability to restore life to its perfect harmonic vibration as it reaches into and works with the etheric field. Crystals, and indeed the rest of the mineral kingdom, embody a conscious desire to work with human cooperation. To regard them, as is so often done, as objects merely of decoration is to ignore their level of intelligence and in fact has a limiting effect on your own development.

In the early civilizations, particularly in Atlantis, there was misuse of electrical and mineral energy based on a conscious desire for control. In present times any such kind of inappropriate use will have immediate repercussions for the user, as the world of minerals has now evolved to a level at which it is no longer a passive force waiting to be used, but is actually aligned to the light with a desire to serve humanity for the highest good. Attempts to violate the integrity of this part of the mineral kingdom are liable to fail drastically, since the cosmic law that human beings are to live in harmony with all natural forces will quickly assert itself.

Something of the Earth is always of the Earth and a crystal or mineral such as mica will continue to resonate with the collective qualities of the group consciousness from which it comes. It is never an isolated form of energy but always part of the whole, just as human beings are themselves part of their own collective field of consciousness, even when appearing to be isolated or emotionally separated from each other. Working with crystal can restore the balance of the

196

human energy field as well as that of the Earth. The special qualities of the crystal have the potential to protect, improve, and empower the environment. By producing an electromagnetic field of intense capacity where needed, and at the same time receiving the input of human intention, they can also be used to shield areas from inharmonious influences.

Using the same inherent energy, your ancestors carved man-made patterns with alternately charged fields upon the granite slabs and uprights of the dolmens and the great burial mounds. Some of these patterns represent solar power, others portray the stones themselves and certain ritual artifacts. They were intended to generate a local supply of electromagnetic energy to assist the departing spirits of the dead to return to their origins in the skies.

Different markings were made to provide energy for initiation and other rites of passage, and to enhance your human ability to communicate with the unseen forces in a reciprocal way. Certain patterns made on the stones were, and still can be, activated by the process of thought or by tracing the design with the hand or eye.

Conversely, dowsable patterns upon the Earth can be created by certain human activities involving higher motivation. Sometimes this is involuntary, as with the spiral force field often found at the baptismal font in ancient churches and in places where spiritual healing is practiced, and with the circular band which invisibly surrounds most sacred sites. Other times it appears by deliberate action. For instance, the medieval Knights Templars imprinted the ground with mystic symbols by the power of thought. Most of the Neolithic dolmens and burial mounds, or their former sites, are linked and carry a man-made pattern, a serpentine line of negative polarity, sometimes with a positive center line. Within the structure you will not find the regular planetary grids, for they have been deliberately removed to free the spirits of the dead from any terrestrial influences to which they might become attached. The serpentine pattern symbolizes and energizes the journey of the soul toward the higher worlds of being; we can liken it to Jacob's ladder, on which angelic help is available at every rung. All these imprints can be dowsed or detected by sensitive human perception, and demonstrate the hidden fields of power around Earth with which you have the ability to cooperate.

Le Vieux Moulin row at Plouharnel

Crystals and minerals are now being brought back into service in a more evolved way than ever before, as well as being artificially made for the storage of information in your current technology. They are a special form of life with a need to work with human intelligence, which is part of their, and your, evolutionary function. As more comprehension filters into the dark recesses of the human mind, the ability to work with all forms of mineral life will be enhanced. You are actually in the process of changing your own vibratory fields, in a development which will literally allow in a wider frequency range of light and make it possible for you to resonate with more of the color spectrum held within the crystal.

Your soul itself can be likened to a crystal with many facets, each facet representing a different incarnation, each a period of work with the chakras in resonance with the subtle variations of color vibrations. Over time every facet of the crystal comes to be polished so that each can in turn reflect the light of the Creator; the process of each incarnation will be completed in this same way. In the incarnation that you are now experiencing it is becoming possible to polish the unfinished or seemingly dark facets of previous lives. This is the final resolution of previous trauma and the transformation of negative energies by the healing of those aspects that were left unfinished. For this it is sometimes useful to return to a place where you spent part of a previous incarnation. By bringing the vitality of your present incarnation to that place, many difficulties carried from the past can be resolved. For this purpose you may be given a sudden recognition and memory of the relevant event and place.

Crystals have the ability to clear stress in the material world. Because they contain such pure vibrations of light they can harmonize the life force, which is itself an expression of light, the illuminating frequencies of the Archangel Michael and the Sun. As you know, within the human body are tiny but essential levels of minerals, the so-called trace elements, which work to balance and harmonize your nutrition and bodily functions. In a similar way the purpose of minerals and crystals in the earth is to keep the balance, to nourish each area and bring a certain energy to it, enabling every part to function as an organic element of the whole.

In the biblical Revelation of Saint John, the Holy City—the New Jerusalem—is described as being built of gold, pearl, and twelve kinds of precious stone. Each one of these special forms of mineral matter has a vibrational quality both symbolic and actual, and will be used to create what has been called a new temple of life, which is synonymous with the purified rainbow body of the spiritual warriors to come.

The twelve gateways of Revelation are a reference to twelve of the Archangels. The twelve stones used in our building of the Holy City represent our higher qualities and what they can contribute to life on Earth; in other words, the Archangelic attributes of which we have already spoken. Gold stands for the spiritual outcome that is purity of the soul. Pearl represents planet Earth in its intention to assimilate and transform the darkness and achieve the purity of light. Each precious stone has a special significance.

Jasper and Release

Jasper, the first precious stone, represents the ability to develop a new perspective in life, which will give humankind an awareness of the manifold attributes of the Creator. These are the primary qualities that manifest through the Archangels, set out in so many spiritual traditions, including the ninety-nine names of God in the Sufi teachings, the Hebrew Kabbalah, and the various attributions of the Hindu pantheon. Jasper clears the subtle energy fields, dispersing energy and not allowing it to cling to the aura. With its capacity to align the spiritual with the material, jasper can help to loosen humanity from the fetters of past incarnations, releasing your potential in the material world. Both the Atlanteans and the Mayan shamans used jasper for protection while experiencing out-of-body travel, and to ensure their safe return. It helped them to stay connected to their physical bodies. Jasper resonates specifically with the heart chakra, linking it with the higher energies of the Source.

Sapphire and Beauty

Sapphire brings a sensitive yet intense feeling of beauty to the new temple of life. Active on several levels, it can attune the user to the intuitive right brain, stilling the ceaseless activity of the left brain and quieting your thoughts. It can help you to realize worldly abundance, as it, too, aligns the spiritual with the physical, drawing whatever is needed into physical reality. This can happen through communication with other realms of existence—the unseen worlds of the elementals and the angels, for example—in a rapport that sapphire will enhance. It can help you realize your true purpose as an individual in the world, by bringing clarity and the ability to make use of higher forces to fulfill those intentions which are for the good of all. Sapphire carries vibrations that encourage the flow of the life force through the chakras, linking them with the Source of life, attuning individual spirit to the eternal spirit, reawakening human energy and enhancing your aura.

Chalcedony and Unity

Through its balancing influence on the spiritual and physical bodies, chalcedony brings a sense of the unity of all beings with the Creator, a feeling of oneness. It transforms emotional disturbances and raises them to a higher level, making you more aware of being a part of "all that is." It encourages the feeling of belonging to a community that is aligned to the highest truth. Chalcedony enables the spirit to be flexible, to adapt to changes in the material world and the differing stages in life. Physically, it unfreezes the human diaphragm by enabling life-enhancing breath to be taken in, and regenerates the body by allowing spirit to permeate it. This improves your ability to receive guidance from the angelic realm, which can be used to create a new and stimulating vision for the future, based on the wisdom accumulated from all your past experiences.

Emerald and Integrity

Emerald assists in the unification of male and female qualities, bringing in joy and the capacity to feel at home in the physical world. It helps to heal the past and prevent flaws in your lineage from developing into negative karmic retribution. It encourages the quality of discernment, instilling loyalty to the Creator, harmony with your own blueprint, and awareness of cosmic laws. The vitality of personal relationships is raised by its use because it activates the power of Love in the heart chakra. The mental body can be protected by emerald's ability to act as a filter for knowledge, letting you assimilate only what is true. The connection with the Source is always maintained and expressed in daily life through your positive actions. Emerald embodies purity of intention, which can be manifested in the material world, raising your aspirations in life to the highest harmonic. It is an anchor for the emotions, providing a firm grounding for human stability.

Sardonyx and Reversing Negativity

The fifth stone of the new temple, sardonyx, illuminates your reason for incarnation on the Earth. It promotes understanding with clarity of intention. Because its presence raises the vibration of a person or place, keeping the lower emotions in check, it is particularly useful when energy levels are low for any reason. Communication with the elementals is enhanced by working with this mineral. There is a strong balance between spirit and matter, fire and earth, since it brings spirit to earth in a grounding way. Use of the active vibrations of sardonyx can reverse the negativity left by the Fall, transcending pollution in the mind and restoring integrity to the human aura. It is a gift for humanity that strengthens your appreciation of nature's abundance and the need to share it unselfishly with others, a process that will also effectively prevent its depletion.

Carnelian and Inspiration

Carnelian brings agreement where there is discord, especially on the spiritual level, allowing you to receive higher inspiration. The connection with your own inner teacher and your soul purpose is activated, helping you to express your innate talents. Any negative energy in the aura is directed toward the light of transformation. Carnelian helps you to hear the messages borne on the wind. It increases your awareness of cosmic and earthly forces, the vibrations of which you may feel in your environment, as former peoples did. It also creates an energy of expansion and growth, stimulating forward movement. Carnelian is a catalyst for healing, giving the angels and the elementals a point of contact within the human being. The use of carnelian in a building produces a harmonious effect and so can be used to enhance your living space; it projects something of the original delight and joy that were present when life first began.

Chrysolite and Prayer

Chrysolite heightens human receptivity at the contemplative level. Awareness of the divine is strengthened because the pineal chakra is activated, bringing light into the unconscious recesses of the mind. Prayer, or communication with the divine, is intensified; true prayer not being a demand but the experience of silence from the other side of time. Chrysolite improves your ability to accept those changes in life, the rites of passage so necessary for growth. It increases understanding of whatever has been obstructing development, helping you return to the blueprint that holds the true pattern of life; it can be used to harmonize the chakras. Eternal values are better recognized, and many blessings can be experienced with this mineral. Chrysolite ennobles the true self, which can acknowledge and celebrate every expression of life, and it blesses the relationship between man and woman.

Beryl and Responsibility

Beryl, like chrysolite, augments that all-important relationship between man and woman by integrating the male and female aspects of the self and opening the intellect to the wisdom of the Creator. It activates the crown and spleen chakras, freeing you from historical or educational limitations and karmic influences. Those who wear beryl find it increases their ability to take personal responsibility for their soul journey, which leads to development of the true self. It strengthens your determination to evolve. Beryl can heal the grief of separation, indeed of all the separations humanity has ever experienced; we include in this the feelings of separation from the Creator, from the Garden, from the truth, and from each other. All these partings can be rejoined and made whole again. The legacy of human separation can be brought to a close and the state of Grace restored.

Topaz and the Law of Attraction

Topaz brings the higher powers of Love to the emotional body, raising the lower emotions by the light of divine Love. It aligns personal will to that of the divine, making the Creator your source of energy at all times, and bringing a greater inner strength into your life. Topaz can turn the destructive turmoil of human emotions into a higher expression of creative inspiration. When as humans you are free from the fixed beliefs of the past, when you start asking questions and begin to take personal responsibility for your evolution, the path you tread may not be familiar but you have the guidance of the angels of truth and light. Topaz is linked with the law of attraction and so helps to manifest whatever is needed for the enhancement of your life. Your desire to serve only the highest good will then come from inspiration, not simply from a sense of duty.

Many curses have been laid upon human lives, and are still. A curse is a work of darkness; we might say that through your negative emotions you have effectively cursed one another from the beginning. Those energies from the past that resonate in the present will not be removed until an individual able to recognize the existence of a curse consciously asks for our angelic help in lifting it. Curses can be transformed into the higher vibrations of Love with the aid of topaz. The stone can also help in releasing ancestral disharmony, healing the hearts of your ancestors and bringing their blessings into the present.

It is as easy to send out negative energy to someone in the form of bad feelings, as it is to send love. Any emotion, whether harmful or loving, attaches itself to the aura of the person and so affects the vibrations of his or her life. Many childhood fairy tales remind you of this. At the present time many curses from the past are being cleared, and you can do this work yourself. Simply ask for angelic assistance to transform any curses that you may have consciously or inadvertently laid upon anyone. You may wish to ask also that curses affecting your own life should be lifted and transformed into light. All of the angelic level will assist in this process, and the Archangel Uriel is particularly helpful here. If not removed by your conscious intention, these harmful wishes will continue to affect your life. It is important that you move forward in freedom and with blessings, unhampered by the past.

Chrysoprase and Ancient Teaching

Chrysoprase encourages an orientation toward the light. It holds within it a strong consciousness of higher energies, attuning the user to the wisdom of many esoteric teachings. The unique qualities of an individual who works with this mineral can be expressed as a true manifestation of the divine. It is a stone of acceptance, the acceptance of the Creator. It replaces judgmental and critical attitudes with total Love. An open mind can then reconnect with the truth and Love of the Creator, developing a positive relationship with Earth and the cosmos. Chrysoprase has a vibration that opposes the dark forces of destruction by working positively with the life force to create new life. It can help to transform your emotions from willful thinking into consciousness of the Christ energy, by which your transition from one stage to another will be eased in a conscious alignment to the light.

Jacinth and Alignment

To those already attuned to the light, jacinth brings the comfort of peace. It brings in intercession from the highest level whenever ancestral healing is required, or negative energy needs to be transformed. It helps to resolve difficult situations and enables individuals to advance in a wholesome way through appropriate understanding and action. Energies are allowed to flow freely, as any blocks to creative action are removed and transformed. This is a mineral with the capacity to align the mental, emotional, spiritual, and physical levels in the harmony of inner knowledge and joy, since it contains the vibrations of the highest order required for human spiritual growth.

You will feel bright and robust under its influence. Those who have been closed to spiritual influence can be opened by working with it; the spirit of life can be directly revealed to them. This stone may be used also to release those earthly spirits who have left their bodies but are trapped just beyond the Earth plane. You can facilitate their release by using jacinth as a focus for angelic energies: ask that a spirit trapped in this way be turned to the redeeming light of the Christ consciousness.

Amethyst and Spiritual Truth

Finally, the gemstone amethyst is a manifestation of the life force itself, which has been represented as the inner path of spirituality in the mystical teachings of the Kabbalah, in Islam, and by the words of Christ and the Buddha. Amethyst revives your need to honor the spiritual truth; it softens hard emotions, changing them to higher feelings. By strengthening the quality of self-rule in each person, amethyst enables you to take responsibility for your own spiritual growth, attuning you to the perfection of the Creator. It has the power to align your chakras, and in doing so provides harmony for those in its presence; the aura will shine and you will release old patterns of negativity. One who wears the amethyst has an extended aura that acts as a protective shield of energy and puts the wearer in closer touch with his or her soul destiny. It maintains a person's spiritual integrity even in situations where it is denied by others.

Gold and Purity

Gold is included in the temple of life for the powerful significance of its strength and purity. As a pure substance and conductor of electricity, its energy may be too strong for certain people, some of whom have even become deranged in their search for it as a form of wealth; such individuals could not cope with its unalloyed strength. It is a symbol, however, of purity and human dignity which, when used by those who are pure in themselves, will align them with their higher qualities, not with the lower emotions. Yet when integrity is lacking, the possession of gold can easily corrupt and unbalance the human persona.

The reference to gold in Revelation indicates that the inhabitants of the Holy City will be incorruptible. They will be "the faithful ones," enlightened and discriminating, fully aware of their bond with the life force. They will have freedom and purity of spirit, they will have been tried and tested, and they will live with joy and Love. Fully in themselves, their will divinely aligned, they will celebrate life with fellow human beings in complete wholeness of heart. In practical terms the use of gold for healing, to harmonize the endocrine system and the chakras, can thus release the residue of old stored trauma and restore the integrity of the human heart. By wearing gold, the pure in heart are able to use the forces that activate their own body to effect the healing of others.

There has always been a mystery surrounding the power of gold. You picture the alchemists of old seeking to transmute base metals into it, and the search for the philosopher's stone is one of those little-understood myths. The philosopher, as one who thinks about life and rational ways of living it, is using his left brain and logical mind. True alchemy, for the philosopher, would make use also of the intuition of his right brain, bringing in a sixth sense through the light in the pineal gland. We can say that the pineal gland is in effect the mysterious philosopher's stone, and that the story is an allusion to the rich potential of that gland in the body. It is the light reaching the pineal gland that links you to the subtle, higher energies of the universe in a process inaccessible to the left brain. In that way "rational human" becomes "wise human," fully empowered and intuitively aware of messages from his or her environment, sensitive to cooperative ways of living in it.

The alchemy of turning base metal into gold symbolizes a raising of the lower human energies to a higher level through inherited wisdom, an old ability to connect with the patterns of the cosmos. It represents the inner quest to turn darkness into light. The end product is purity, the indestructible quality of gold that, even when melted down and re-formed, cannot be destroyed. It is time for the symbolism of the old stories to be understood by your conscious mind; they have been lurking in your subconscious for too long.

Pearl and Innocence

Pearl, last of the components of the New Jerusalem, connects the wearer with the profundity of spiritual teachings. It can enhance your intuitive access to the wisdom of the masters. As a pearl is formed by a disturbance in a living organism, it symbolizes that wisdom and purity can be achieved by working positively through the difficulties and challenges which life provides. Thus the foundations of the new temple are to be the accumulated wisdom of all humanity's experiences.

As a gentle healer of the heart, pearl is also a reminder that everything is ultimately in service to the Creator, that a particle of grit, or an impurity, can become something of beauty to be cherished. Whatever is considered unclean can be purified, restoring it to a state of Grace. Pearl harmonizes and purifies both male and female energies, leading to feelings of greater unity. Those who work with its energy and with spiritual guidance can resolve all ancestral issues. Innocence in its most powerful and incorruptible form radiates from this stone.

All crystal and mineral forms of matter come from and are closely connected to the spiritual consciousness that surrounds the Earth. Accordingly, they are to be used as generators in the task of raising human consciousness toward that of the Creator. They have the capacity to deliver humanity from enslavement to its own limitations—from a restricted involvement in life, to a consciously higher level of being, to a greater recognition of the expansiveness of nature in the unseen world, or what you sometimes call the paranormal.

The human aura that surrounds you and includes the energy fields of your chakras is the electrically charged bridge that links you with other, invisible, living worlds. This subtle connecting web, when you are in harmony with it, can bring a great feeling of serenity, helping each individual to become fully incarnate. Your chakras are in resonance with the elegant gift of crystal power, which can bring about the repair of disconnected attitudes and fragmented selves, allowing even the self-saboteur of personality to be pacified and integrated. Social stresses will be alleviated; a newly structured society will be developed. In the promise of the new temple of life, human beings of integrity and wisdom will each become a temple to the light.

Living Crystals

Quite often, when giving people healing treatments, I have used crystals whenever appropriate, but for a long time I was skeptical about their ability to help. I then had some experiences that changed my attitude.

Once I was working with a young woman who had come to me for healing and guidance. She brought with her a large chunk of rose tourmaline. She was separating from her boyfriend, and the crystal was one of their treasured possessions. Each of them wanted it. The question was, who was to have it?

She put forward the idea of cutting the stone in half. There was an immediate response from the crystal, which I heard and she felt. It said quite clearly, "I don't belong to either of you! It is the other way round. You belong to me, since crystal intelligence is much higher than that of humans. However, I am willing to work with you. Halving me will not do me any harm, but it will not serve any purpose, because your motive is possession, which shows no respect, only a desire for ownership. You can share me, and I will spend time with each of you in turn."

The surprise we both felt at this revelation was enough. The young woman decided there and then to share the crystal, turn and turn about, with her friend.

One day another young woman came in for a healing session. She was in considerable pain as she lay down on the treatment couch. This time I was distinctly told not to involve myself with the healing but to make use of my piece of amethyst. Rather doubtfully I placed it at the critical point on her body and sat back to let it work. After about twenty minutes, I was told that was long enough and removed the stone. The patient was transformed—she got up laughing, full of energy, and after an enthusiastic conversation she left, walking normally again.

I always cleanse any crystal after it has been used for healing. On that occasion I was surprised to find that it took a full six weeks to clear the amethyst. A few days after the cleansing was finished, I received a letter of thanks from the young woman saying that she had been free of pain for six weeks. It was the crystal's vibrational frequency and its connection with higher cosmic power that had helped her, activated, as seems to be necessary, by human intention.

Sometime later we moved house and I packed up my crystals in a box. For several months I was unable to find them despite looking everywhere possible. Then one day I saw the box in a place where I knew I had looked, an obvious place where I would certainly have noticed it even if I were not consciously looking. The crystals and their box had been spirited away in a mysterious fashion, and spirit had decided to return them. I was very happy to have found them, but after unwrapping them carefully I put them aside again without clearing or reprogramming them, intending to do so later. A few days of this neglectful attitude was enough to cause my loud-voiced angel to pay a visit, waking me in the middle of the night to ask in a booming and remonstrative voice, "Well, now you have found your crystals, why aren't you using them?"

—*Natasha*

Interior of dolmen at Rondossec

CHAPTER 10

Restoration

The world must refind its heart.

—Thomas Mann

The objective now for our human family on planet Earth is the healing of the human heart through the restoration of Grace, the Grace of living in harmony with cosmic law. This agreeable state of being will acknowledge that the divine Source of nourishment upon which your planet depends is neither female nor male but embraces and transcends both genders. When the divine feminine and masculine attributes are united in every aspect of human life, then man, woman, and the Creator will be perceived as a new and undistorted holy trinity.

This alchemical unification can occur only within each individual, by the balancing of your personal energies. Then, when true spirituality returns through your sensitive and positive response to life, the necessary equilibrium between two individuals of the "opposite" sex can be achieved.

Our intention for human life is a surrender to the divine will in an integration of all those dualities which for you are seemingly opposed, such as good and evil, love and hate, male and female, spiritual and physical. By being in love with life, by developing your sensitivity and your feelings, you can learn what it is to be truly human, to live and love at the level of your own empowerment, free from false emotions and fixed expectations.

True feelings that are suppressed by the rational habits of the intellect emerge as negative emotions that are so often destructive in their expression. True feelings come from wholeness of heart and an understanding of what is love and what is not. Negative emotions come from a heart that is wounded.

In the restoration of truly human values, and indeed as part of the process of evolution, the vitality of life itself will break all those old patterns that are not life enhancing. You can see the cracks appearing now in the changing face of your social structures, as the unwholesome veneer is peeled off to make way for a new order.

As the human body becomes attuned to higher frequencies and you strive to find your own note and bring new vibrations into your lives, you will find that your tune can never be the same as anyone else's. This is because each one of you has a unique pattern as an individual. Only when your tune and your light resonate with the harmonies of the universe will you find harmony within yourselves.

We wish to prepare you for what lies ahead for your planet by first explaining that a combination of cosmic and human energies is calling future events into being. The blend of energies on the Earth and within each individual will alter; wherever there is an imbalance there will be a corrective impulse, leading finally to equilibrium.

All the pollution upon the planet, in its oceans and atmosphere, is but a reflection of, and is created by, the presence of pollution in the human mind. There must be a change of mind. There is a close inter-dependence between the healing of the planet and the healing of humanity; as you become whole, so will the planet. Since change will take place both upon the body of the planet and at the cellular level in humans, you will experience disturbances. If your inner disturbances go unresisted, there may be less need for the external ones.

A greater understanding of how the forces of negativity manifest and express themselves within each of you is an essential requirement for the progression of life on Earth and for the evolution of the human soul. Negativity shows itself in the guise of politics and finance, religion and morality, science and education, medicine and many techno-logical advancements. Wherever there are institutions without a true spiritual center there will be opportunities for corruption, manipulation, and domination by those who wish to exercise control without integrity by imposing unworthy standards upon you.

The shadows are particularly evident in your financial institutions. Monetary gain is a false priority but provides the motivation for action or nonaction in your lives; that is to say, it encourages the greed of acquisition or the selfishness of parsimony. It is seldom recognized that because the energy of the Creator is everywhere, it is also present in money. Divine energy is therefore involved in financial matters, and transactions which fail to honor the integrity of the individual or do not serve the highest good in humanity will inevitably be followed by other events that will serve to redress the imbalance.

However, if worldly decisions—whether personal or governmental—are made by the light of cosmic truth, such honesty will have a powerful, positive effect on other people, freeing some from the conformist pressures of the social order. Others who are still enslaved by false goals may be unable to adjust to a new transparency, and their time here will be limited. When humans feel a conflict between the Creator's will and their own and do not know which way to turn, there is often a fearful resistance to change. Your life cannot flow creatively if you are unable to find the direction of the highest good. Even when you find it, you may experience difficulties in following it if there is resistance in you.

Just as you can experience blockages in your own life that are emotional, creative, spiritual, or physical, so too can the Earth hold energies that can become blocked, since it has to absorb all the human pain and sufferings of the past and present. These thwarted energies need release and transformation through a healing of wounds and their underlying origins. Planet Earth may be sick but will not die, however, as its purpose has not yet been completed. As an essential component in the totality of the life of the universe, it will undergo inevitable changes in its physical evolution, as it has so often in the past. Each major change signifies both spiritual and physical development and marks a new phase in the life of the planet and its inhabitants.

All the energy that flows from the thoughts in your minds rever-
berates into the environment, expanding, changing, or constricting
it. When more light can enter your minds, you will develop a greater
awareness by simply linking in light with others. For those of you whose
destiny is to remain on the planet, this will build a more holistic life.
It is part of the process of restoration of Grace, which has been made
possible on Earth because of the presence and teachings of the
masters. They brought to you all the possibilities of experiencing an
enriched life through spiritual attunement, through gaining awareness
of the higher levels of spiritual consciousness which are so necessary
to transcend the density of earthly life. It is time that the simple—
and at the same time complex—truth become known to you all. Let
us say that in this relearning, even those who have experienced total
separation from the Source will be able to feel themselves part of a
loving universe.

If every physical action, every mental decision, can be imbued with
a sense of the sacred, then life will become whole once more. The tasks
which you may consider small or unimportant, even boring, such as
peeling the potatoes or washing the floor, then become imbued with
spirit and make a contribution to the quality of your life. You will be
creating and working in sacred space. Many of those endeavoring to
lead a contemplative life of the spirit, perhaps as a monk or nun, have
had to spend many hours doing menial tasks that were intended to
ground them and prevent spiritual pride. We do not say that it is always
necessary, but it did not separate them from the enlightenment they

sought and often brought inspiration to their lives. Honest work is service.

The sacredness of life is not an optional extra, to be accepted or rejected at will; it needs to be brought into every aspect of daily life. All life is sacred and blessed by the Creator. When humans bless something they have created, the Creator is also bestowing a blessing, a concerted act that brings in the higher spiritual energies.

Earth is a place where human consciousness has had to evolve by a baptism, not so much of fire or water but of dense matter, the immersion causing separation from spirit. Now and in the coming times it will continue to evolve toward reunification with spirit, drawing it back into the material level, returning to an awareness of what has been there all along, but unnoticed. Life on Earth cannot continue without the consciousness of spirit to sustain it.

Many of Earth's inhabitants, including much of the present animal life, will leave the planet if pollution, in its widest sense, continues to contaminate all that is sacred. Earth, as we have said, has a built-in capacity to restore itself without human help, but for the evolutionary development of human souls active cooperation with your planet is essential. Only those human souls with sufficiently enlarged awareness and love in their hearts will be returning in a new incarnation to resume this work with the light. Those who are unwilling to accept cosmic law and do not wish to cooperate will not be returning—by their own choice, they will move elsewhere to work out their evolutionary process.

Cromlech at Le Ménec

Freedom from dogmatic systems of belief, from resistance to change, will enable you to be more flexible in accepting the journey of each soul, your own soul's journey and that of others, without making judgments. The Creator does not judge. The Creator encompasses all, loves all. It is only humans, in their arrogance, who are judgmental, because of the self-righteousness and the fear in their hearts. Religions were born of doctrine and fear, not of the inspiration of the original teachings, not of the understanding of the Creator's cosmic truth, nor of any true awareness of the journey of the soul.

Much human fear has come from the concept of original sin that has overlaid the words of the Master Jesus. What could be more demoralizing than to feel you were already a sinner at the moment of birth? What more powerful a way to lower self-esteem? Doctrine of this sort has made so many people feel vulnerable and ashamed, separated from the Creator, and hence willing to accept domination by others. It is a concept totally at odds with the cosmic truth, which is that each human being has a soul that is part of the Creator. Your soul breathes spirit into your human frame and gives you life. At the death of the body, the spirit rejoins the soul on its continuing journey to the light, taking with it the lessons learned from that particular incarnation. The soul is eternal. Although it cannot die, it can become so wounded by worldly experiences and by failing to transcend the sufferings of the body that it is unable to return to the light. After many years or incarnations of hardship, the spirit sometimes retreats. The light goes out of a person's life and cannot be found again. Even in those circumstances it is still possible, with much courage and our help, to call back the spirit to become fully incarnate and once again take responsibility for its own evolution.

Many of those presently incarnating on Earth have not previously experienced a life on this planet, and these souls have a very strong spirit presence because they have no history of suffering or emotional woundings. They are filled with enthusiasm for life's radiance and will not easily allow themselves to be led away from the truth. There are also souls who will resist to the last the process of transformation, testing not only their own strength but yours too. Every human being has to take responsibility for the transformation of whatever darkness has clouded his or her mind with judgments of what is right and what is wrong, who is acceptable and who is not. Whatever appears as negative has to be embraced to be transformed, however difficult this may seem; it is part of the equation of unity.

Remember that all acts against humanity come from the shadow side of yourselves. If there is a shadow in anyone's heart, then someone, somewhere, will pick it up and act it out. Shadows are the result of separation, rejection, and fear—fear of not enough love, food, or money. Shadows are the good that did not happen, the love that was not given. Love is the most sustaining energy upon your planet and therefore the one that has been the most distorted. As a result, many people lack that essential form of nourishment, unaware of what they are missing.

There are many hungry for love, for food, and for their basic needs. Without those, talk of the expression of talents and creativity is meaningless. Even where there is sufficient food, it so often lacks the nourishment of love and it is chemically compromised. The life of the soil in which your food crops grow is being seriously weakened by the use of chemicals. Food that is produced in this manner absorbs the manmade toxins and is further corrupted by processing with chemical additives. Increasingly it is transported hundreds of miles from its place of origin, and it is losing wholeness and vitality. Truly you no longer dine with love, nor honor the land that feeds you. Restoration of food health is essential to prevent the continuation of serious damage to humanity's health. The life of the soil is also impoverished by the growing of extractive crops for monetary gain rather than local subsistence.

This makes for great hardship for many people who work the land but get little benefit from it. We can say, too, that all misuse of the land creates difficulties for the nature spirits, whose life vibrations are out of harmony with your present practices.

In some areas, precious land has been laid to waste by the removal of forests, some even sterilized by its use for the testing of weapons of destruction, or by the disposal of toxic substances. No human technology can reverse such actions, and the natural process of regeneration, in terms of human life, is a lengthy one.

Although many of you are aware of the effects these unthinking actions will have on the quality and future of life on Earth, you do not realize that they also affect the rest of the cosmos. The evolution and health, even the survival, of other planets depends in many ways upon what happens on Earth. Those who exist in other dimensions cannot afford to lose you or your planet to human stupidity and lack of conscious awareness.

The evolutionary process was hindered once before in your history, when free will was abused by those whose one objective was to exercise control. Free will now is limited; you have only the power of choice. You can choose to work with cosmic law, or against it by deliberately continuing to upset the natural balance. There are choices to be made upon other planets, but they are within the natural order and do not disturb the pattern of evolution.

Perhaps you can see that the restoration of Grace we are urging does not affect only those with a physical human body. It influences every level of life, visible and invisible; animal, vegetable, and mineral, elemental and devic; and even our angelic realm.

Give thanks for the abundance that is provided when you cooperate with natural forces. The very act of thankfulness nourishes and invigorates the natural environment. If there is too much misuse of land, uncontrolled genetic interference, or excessive use of chemicals, there will be no abundance to be thankful for. Genetic manipulation, for instance, makes for a distorted soul energy, or "essence," because the Creator is not present in the process. Potentially destructive forces are being released, which, like physical pollution, will inevitably lead to the sickness and death of much of the planet's life.

The intention of the Creator is for planet Earth to sound its own note in harmonic resonance with the other planets. Each has its own musical sound and vibratory rate, so that the whole solar system can merge into and become part of the grand cosmic orchestra. And yes, the music of the spheres does exist—and many of you are beginning to attune to it.

But the sounds that the Earth is presently emitting are those of suffering, and we are not enjoying the disharmony. It may have other unwelcome effects. We must warn you that if the present disturbances continue for long, it is likely that your planet's emanations will pull in an asteroid of some considerable force. As a prophecy, this means that it is not an inevitable event, and we can see the possibility of diminishing the impact or preventing it. At the same time there is a very real danger of calling such an event into being.

It is actually possible for you to raise the vibrations of humanity through love for the Earth and each other, in an affinity with what we would call the great cosmic consciousness. More positive patterns of energy coming from sufficient numbers of people on your planet can reduce negativity, and in that way modify the severity of any asteroid impact.

There are people whose unhappiness is so great that they would almost welcome a destructive event, expecting it to bring an end to their suffering. It would not, since the spirit continues and will evolve not through inaction, but through the making of conscious and constructive decisions. What such people can do is to stop feeling sorry for themselves, accept responsibility, and transform their pain into love. One possible way for this to happen is to develop a new relationship with the Earth, particularly by recognizing the importance of the sacred sites in your locality. The more the links with the Source of all life are restored at such special places, the less will fear control your lives and the more your hearts will open to love. This is one of the ways your own inner healing can take place alongside that of the planet.

In recent history, the markers of many sacred sites have been destroyed, the stones deliberately broken up or removed. Such actions were often a deliberate attempt to separate people from the power of the Creator. They were based on fear of the natural world, rather than on the respect and empathy once customary among pagan peoples who felt they were a part of nature and did not attempt to dominate it. For them everything was sacred, part of the honor due to the Creator and creation. Although those peoples were integrated with their environment—some still are in remote areas—they were not attuned to the angelic forces, realms higher than themselves. With an acceptance of their place in nature and the cosmos, in the observance of planetary cycles and patterns of weather, they achieved a satisfactory, even beautiful relationship with the lower worlds of plants and animals, and always a link with the devic realm. They needed the message of Christ in its original simplicity, not the missionary zeal that told them their traditions were wrong. To increase their awareness and help raise all life to a higher level, they needed to continue their work with the essential lower elements while bringing in the higher spiritual forces.

Unfortunately for humankind, this raising of consciousness did not happen. Paganism was suppressed by organized religion instead of evolving from an animistic level to increasing empathy with the higher worlds. This reduced the energetic activity of the environment, putting a stop to conscious cooperation with nature by those best fitted for it.

The megalith builders were well aware that natural forces were concentrated at certain places. They knew the power of sound as they intoned, chanted, and danced the processional ways in their community rituals. This manner of spiritual alignment is still possible, although we have had to close down a number of the sacred places during times of conflict, or when the energy there was being misused. At such places no nature spirits are present, but devic guardians still remain, awaiting the moment of reactivation.

We cannot overemphasize the importance of reopening these sites and restoring their vital purpose. With a conscious intention you can do this now by calling for our angelic help and devic participation. It is work that can be done simply and lovingly by any of you, but remember that it carries considerable responsibility, as the Earth can hold much negativity and darkness. To counteract the darkness requires firmness of spirit; the task should be undertaken not in a foolhardy way, but with due preparation, lightness of heart, and our support. In this way you will effectively enhance the light of the Creator on the planet.

Ever since your principal religions became power based rather than spiritually oriented, the knowledge of the power held within these sacred places has been restricted to those whose main objective was to control their followers. But now the organizations which built their shrines on these ancient sites, drawing upon the energies there to fuel their own credo, are finding that their influence is drawing to a close.

At this time many people throughout the world are becoming fascinated by the standing stones at the sacred places. In this surge of interest a deep memory has begun to surface of the connection with the Source, as such people are drawn, like filings to a magnet, to seek inner harmony there. By gathering together and joyfully and respectfully activating those sites which may now be reopened, it is not too much to say that you will be helping the restoration of Earth's balance with the solar system, and therefore contributing to the harmony of the universe. The energy of those sleeping places needs to be blessed and reconsecrated on awakening, so that it cannot be abused by those who are not yet able or willing to work with the light. Such interaction will ease the flow of the solar currents along the terrestrial pathways we laid out so long ago, strengthening their activity at other sacred sites and restoring health and fertility to many dead areas of the land.

The human heartbeat is the first sound a baby hears as it leaves the world of spirit and takes form in the mother's womb. It is the pulse of life on Earth, a gentle sound that echoes earthly rhythms. It unites human beings with the spirit of Earth and awakens your own hearts to the presence of soul.

In the past various instruments have been used to make your calls to the Earth spirit: the harp, drums, the Tibetan horn, conch shells, the didgeridoo, all with the aim of bringing people closer to it. Now these sounds of music, and especially the toning of the human voice, can be combined with Grace and joy to harmonize your own spiritual energy with that of the angels and devas. Such simple ceremonies will refresh and rejuvenate your lives and reactivate the sites.

Remember to call us in. Acknowledge the guardians of place, ask for the presence of the Archangels, the angelic host, as you feel may be appropriate. We will always support your intention to restore the harmony of your planet.

A Sacred Site

At the beginning of our quest Natasha and I had no detailed map of Carnac and were working from a tourist brochure, which showed only the main monuments. After taking in the alignments and paying a visit to the nearby audiovisual display in a modern building by the carpark, we drove around a while to look at some of the less-visited dolmens, the tomb and temple structures. I was particularly drawn to a hamlet called Crucuno, which has a large dolmen and, not far away, an unusual megalithic feature of quadrilateral shape. We soon found the dolmen, rearing up against one of the village houses in a rather sad little grouping. For many years it had served as a henhouse and cycle shed, and once, apparently, as the home of some poor villager. The quadrilateral was not so straightforward. We made one attempt to locate it, without success.

On our next visit, we walked down a muddy lane through the fields, until at length over the hedgerow we sighted the gray granite megaliths, several fields away and obscured by trees. There was no obvious route to them, so we climbed over a gate, crossed one field and then another, to find ourselves blocked by a barbed-wire fence and hedge. We struggled through the wire, Natasha protesting by now, then over another fence and a very wet ditch—and there it was, a row of great stones forming one side of the quadrilateral, large and heavily choked with prickly gorse and small trees. As a national monument it was very neglected, though someone had cleared parts of it with a scythe and most of the upright stones were accessible.

Once inside, we realized that this was the sacred place our spirit guide had told us of during our last session. It had been closed down by the angels because of human misuse during the armed struggle in Brittany which followed the French Revolution. We had the responsibility of reactivating it, he had said, but without mentioning how. We checked for the usual reaction from the stones, which normally in such an enclosure, resonate positive and negative from one to the next. Nothing, it was shut down, dead. We debated what to do and decided to call upon the angelic host. Then we each walked slowly around the perimeter in opposite directions, touching each stone in turn and asking that it be brought back to life. We met finally; I checked with the pendulum, and yes, there was a reaction, one monolith positive, the next negative and so on, right around the rectangle of the twenty-two stones. To our surprise and gratification, the devas and the nature spirits had returned, as though by the magic of the angels: eight devas, seventeen nature spirits, and as we have come to expect, a single goblin. We easily found the footpath back, over an unobtrusive stile and onto the lane.

Crucuno quadrilateral is aligned east and west; the long sides point to the equinox sunsets, while midsummer sunrise and midwinter sunset are marked by the diagonals. Along its southern edge runs a solar band of energy, enabling it to collect and transform solar power, the life force for the natural kingdoms of Earth.

On a later visit we passed through the village again. It too seemed to have been rejuvenated; flowers had appeared in the gardens, new houses were under construction, and craftsmen were working to restore a fine old property overlooking the dolmen. Life had returned.

—Hamilton

Dolmen at Crucuno

CHAPTER 11

Talents and Creativity

If you bring forth what is within you, what you bring forth will save you. If you do not bring forth what is within you, what is within you will destroy you.

—Jesus, the Gospel of Thomas

This is the time for the unique qualities of each man, woman, and child, of every race, to begin to be recognized in the expression of their full creative power. Your individual talents, your creative qualities, are not exactly God-given as some of you think, but have actually been chosen by you in order to manifest the abundance of the Creator in a particular way. Using its freedom of choice, your spirit selected certain talents to bring into your physical existence and to use in exploring the dimensions of your world.

You have earned these talents through many incarnations of working to develop them. In those previous lifetimes you may have been a worker in wood, stone, or metal, a singer or maker of music, perhaps a poet, a painter of icons, or a shepherd who played the flute to his flock.

Creativity covers many activities, and each person usually has more than one skill. Whatever you have learned to do well in each incarnation enriches you and is yours to access and develop in the next incarnation if you so wish.

It saddens your friends in spirit when we see that so many of you have forgotten you were born with innate talents that are intended for you and your fellow humans to enjoy. So many of you have lost your original vision, the plan of your life, because your education has been designed to fit you into the norms of society, but not to develop your abilities as unique individuals. Some of what we would call the most important areas of study are scarcely even mentioned in the general education of the young; for example, the human relationship and interdependence with the planet Earth itself and its animal, vegetable, and mineral life, the natural science of astronomy, the planetary energies, the effect of form as it influences the quality of life in design and architecture. Above all, the arts of music and painting are treated as extras and not included as a main component of education. The aim is normality, ordinariness, which replaces the development of personal abilities with pressure to conform to what is acceptable in the current society.

As Krishnamurti said, "Society's function is to limit the individual, to hold him within the boundary of respectability." And as you know, within the confines of respectability there are repressions that can emerge as very unrespectable at times.

Certainly the type of society which has developed on Earth creates a fear of individuality, a reluctance to be different from the crowd—a definite tribal or herd mentality. It was hoped that by now you would all have outgrown the tribe and become individuals, fulfilled in your own creativity. But the patterns of success are expected to fit whatever conventions are accepted at the time. Ideas that threaten the status quo are rejected, even within the artistic and scientific communities supposedly dedicated to truth. Certain people are groomed to be "successful" and raised up in society as cultural icons, but are easily removed from their pedestal if they challenge the establishment or overstep the norm. There are many examples. We think of Socrates the philosopher, accused of disrespect of the traditional gods and required to end his life life, and of Galileo, condemned for asserting that Earth revolves around the Sun. Such significant figures can and often have become puppets in the hands of the institutions that raised them up.

However, success in a public role does not indicate that a person is on the best path for the evolution of his or her soul. If you lose touch with your vision, for whatever reason, you lose your way in life and can then be influenced by those who would like to use your talents and energies for their own ends.

New ways to the truth have had to be found. By choosing a path within the established order of society—by working from inside— certain people have succeeded in bringing in new understanding, which eventually becomes acceptable. New ideas are disturbing, because they mean changing previous attitudes, giving up the comfort of the status quo in, for instance, science or teaching. There is a great reluctance for anyone to admit errors and lose face.

New insights that dare to introduce new dimensions in art have been found by artists experimenting with light, color, and form. They have also been found by musicians and composers who have played with new harmonies of sound, by scientists who have made new discoveries, and by poets who have found new significance in language which can illuminate and touch the soul. All of these acts of creativity are ways of expressing the divine nature of the Creator.

Many of these great luminaries have been spurned. Often years after their rejection, the truth of their ideas has been recognized and accepted as being of benefit to humanity. Such original minds have a simplicity of soul that, often in vain, expects the world to rejoice at their revelations and welcome them as stepping stones on the road to enlightenment. The French scientist Jacques Benveniste was not honored for proving that the structure of water, as is held in homeopathy, carries a vibratory memory of other substances and phenomena; on the contrary, he was derided by his peers and dismissed.

Your own fulfillment requires that your talents be identified and expressed creatively within this present incarnation. Their development is necessary for the full enjoyment of your life; without it you will have difficulty finding your niche in the world.

The Creator does not allow anyone to come from spirit into physical form without the essential equipment for a life on Earth. Nobody incarnates without a talent of some sort. Those with an obvious affliction who appear to have no talent upon which to draw may well have the ability to bring out love in others—that is indeed a gift. Lives of suppressed talent can culminate in one final life, a distortion in which the lessons that could have been learned with joy are taken in with suffering. Some of those with severe disabilities have drawn this pattern to them because they will no longer need to reincarnate on Earth; they have gathered every fragment of negativity from previous lives to work with all the problems at once. This not only is their contribution to life but also offers a way of learning for others. In a similar way, the distinct races of earlier times had collective talents which were intended to enrich the whole spectrum of human life. Those qualities now are diffused in the national characteristics which have tended to develop within the boundaries of your various countries.

Parents attempt, with what they feel are the best of intentions, to direct their offspring into respectable work, normal jobs, careers in which they will be well paid. How often have we heard you say, "Oh, but there's no money in trying to be creative." This has become a thought-form powerful enough to prevent many people from following their destiny, which, if they trusted in it, would bring them what they needed.

True creative expression is a cord that links you directly with the Creator, who is the Source of all creativity. It is a powerful tool with which your religious and political leaders have often felt uncomfortable, preferring to repress its free expression, since that leads in the direction of individual freedom. It is precisely this that will ultimately make your leaders redundant, along with the unimaginative institutions that they represent.

If your talents are not expressed in some creative way, however, the energy of blocked potential will turn against your physical body and may well manifest negatively as an illness. When that energy cannot be expressed positively it usually becomes destructive; your planet has witnessed this in its most extreme form in the massacres of the past and present. These represent human creative energy reversed, an energy so suppressed, so distorted, that it can be expressed only in conflict, the polarity between victim and oppressor.

You have been conditioned to believe that suffering is good for the soul, when the opposite is true. It is joy that is good for the soul, and you seldom realize that suffering is merely one expression of blocked creative energy. It can be transformed through creative activities that go to the root of the blockage and will open the way to your healing and fulfillment.

There are those who seem to be expressing themselves in a creative way but become seriously ill. This may be because they have drawn upon a talent and used it to inflate their own ego or personality and so are not letting the forces of creation flow freely. If the artist, the writer, and the musician do not make of themselves a channel, then the energy cannot flow *through* them but will simply flow *from* them. Such illness also may occur because certain underlying issues have not been addressed and the illness makes it possible to confront them.

All energy, in fact, needs appropriate expression. Your special abilities serve a purpose beyond supporting your daily needs. Your talents are to resonate with the harmony and beauty of the planets, and need especially to echo the rhythms and recurrent patterns of life on Earth. Whatever you are able to do, it needs to be expressed in terms of the highest human potential, yet remain firmly related to the physical frame-work of Earth. It is a basic function of human beings to work, create ideas, and make things, and in this you are truly co-creators.

Humanity's first and most important need is to feel able to com-municate with the Creator, to know that there is a personal inner link which can provide direct experience. The second most important need is to communicate that experience in a constructive way to other human beings. If that first need is met, conversing with other people will be at a higher level than is usually experienced, and it will be sensitive to the real needs of each person.

The universe abounds in creative energy, which is also spiritual energy. If that spiritual energy is grounded in human beings by the exercise of their creative talents in an inspired form, then that same energy can be the incentive for others to develop better relationships with the Creator, with one another, and with all forms of life.

It is often the case that your creative work follows a fixed formula, adopting concepts from the left side of the brain and lacking spon-taneity. This cannot be called true use of your talents. Too much reliance on the dragon of the intellect can be another underlying cause of ill-ness, a state of imbalance in which full expression of the right side of the brain has been thwarted.

True creative expression requires a conscious link with the power of the universe that makes you a transformer of cosmic energy. In the combined expression of individual and universal truth, this is co-creativity, the vital part of creativity. It is a way to connect with the realm of ideas which already exist at an etheric level. All possibilities are inherent in you and are simply waiting to be translated into form.

The true creative artist distills information from the universe and produces something unique, a fragment that will reflect both a personal perspective and something of the divine essence. It is essential to train and develop all the senses for use in this process so that you do not merely develop a skill without content. Sensitivity, in its full meaning, enables the magic and beauty of spirituality to be imparted, embodied, in the making of the work, whether it is music, words, art, architecture, or inspired craftsmanship of whatever kind.

The expression of talents serves to raise the levels of both macrocosm and microcosm; the joy which the application of talents gives to you, as an individual, gives a stronger sense of identity of the self as part of the whole.

Every act of creation necessitates the appropriate balancing of energies. It requires the cooperation of your spiritual backup team, enlightened souls or angelic entities. You cannot succeed at every level of manifestation, practical, aesthetic, and inspirational, without calling in a balanced combination of all the higher energies that are available to you.

As Archangels, we are an integral part of the structure of the whole, intended to serve as the link between the human and the divine. In the future it will be essential to call upon us, consciously and more frequently, to oversee and lend our energies to every project that humans intend to be positively beneficial to the planet.

There has long been an inherent lack of clarity around the purpose of human life. This uncertainty, the feeling of not being able to follow your own path, is left over from those times when a fixed class structure and rigid social conventions made it hard to follow any personal destiny. Though these restrictions still resonate strongly in the present, you will begin to find that you are directed onto your own journey. Choices will need to be made which will enable you to develop new talents, finding opportunities to seize them and ways to make better use of older ones.

In all this the tree is a powerful symbol for each of you. The roots are where your talents lie like buried treasure, protected and nourished by the richness of the soil; the branches, reaching out, are the support for your talents, which flower among the leaves in a continuous cycle of growth. As the higher and lower energies are taken in and circulated, you are enabled to receive inspiration and give it expression in a practical way.

Inspiration and dignity will return to your lives when you discover what your talents are and learn to work with them. If you fail to do this, it will signal for you, as Chief Seattle once said in another context, "the end of living, and the beginning of survival." This has surely been experienced many times already, and it is important that the pattern be reversed. If the soil under the tree is rich in earthly nourishment and the air around it is empowered by spirit, that pattern will be reversed.

A Goblin Too Far

It was a fine, sunny day in February, and although there was a wind it was not very cold. Hamilton and I were climbing Trencrom Hill in Cornwall with our friends Hamish and Ba and their dog, Ross. From the summit you can see the English Channel on one side and the Bristol Channel on the other. Trencrom is on a solar line and a Jupiter line, each linking it to the great rock of St. Michael's Mount, which can be clearly seen looming up in the distance, just off the shore.

The Sun was glinting on tiny pieces of crystal on the track as we walked up. "Well, you must be very special people," said Ba, "because only rarely does Trencrom yield a crystal to those it welcomes." She picked one off the path and handed it to us.

With a rare enthusiasm for exercise, Ross bounded past and threw himself upon a pile of rocks at the top. "This is the energy focus of Trencrom," said Hamish, and he called to the dog to come down lest the energies affect him. Ross ignored him, which was unusual. Reaching the top some time after Ross, we clambered up to the energy point ourselves and found a triangular arrangement of stones beside a large rock. Hamilton began to dowse for the presence of devas and nature spirits. "That's odd," he said. "There's around forty devas here and some nature spirits, but no goblin; there's always one goblin."

"Try over here," said Hamish, striding toward another impressive rock formation a few yards away. Hamilton followed and checked. "Yes," he said, "he's here, but all alone and not in a good state. He's become separated from the nature spirits."

There was a silence during which I could sense the goblin huddled under the rocks. Then Hamish said, "Well, the energy point used to be here, but it shifted to where it is now," and as we looked at him in anticipation, he said, "There was a Druid ceremony. I was being initiated, and the energy center just moved suddenly a few yards away, to over there," and he looked at the spot where Ross was still sitting on top of the rock. Whatever happened during the ceremony caused a shift of the focal point, which left the goblin on his own. With a less dense light-body than humans, goblins can see us but do not like to show themselves. They cannot see the nature spirits although they are aware of their presence. Nature spirits have even less dense light-bodies but can sometimes be perceived by those of a certain sensitivity, especially in places where the veil is unusually thin.

Perplexed by the goblin's plight, we continued our walk, finding a beautiful spring of clear water under a rockface, completely hidden just below the highest point of the hill and accessible only by squeezing through a cleft in the granite. This spring was evidently the water source for the early inhabitants, the stony remains of whose small, round houses could be seen scattered about, protected by a wall.

Still thinking about what went wrong or what caused the separation and how we could help, we found ourselves on the downward path. Crystals still glittered at us and we picked up two or three tiny ones, feeling they were gifts from the guardians of the hill.

When we got home to Dartmouth, and after some "tuning in," we thought it appropriate to call on the energies of the Archangel Michael, the Christ consciousness, and the angelic host—leaving nothing to chance. A few days later, donning warm coats, we went onto the nearby cliffs where a tall standing stone overlooks the sea. Standing against it, we invoked those presences and asked for their help. The Sun came out from behind the clouds, and as it shone upon the sea and us, we felt lighter, knowing that help had come and the connection at Trencrom was somehow, miraculously, restored.

A few days later we had a letter from Ba, who had gone up on the hill at the same time we were asking for help. She had talked to the nature spirits and asked for their aid in making all well again, and felt that they had heard and understood. They know well how essential the goblin's work is at each sacred site, holding down the light-energy in readiness for its transformation by the devas.

Between us all, order had been restored at Trencrom Hill.

—Natasha

CHAPTER 12

The Journey of the Soul

There is no death, only a change of worlds.

—Chief Seattle

As a person puts on new garments, giving up the old ones, the soul similarly accepts new material bodies, giving up the old and useless ones.

—The Bhagavad Gita

W hen we speak of the journey of the soul, we are referring merely to that part of its progression which involves incarnations in a human body, although some of you can recall that your soul has also experienced life in other dimensions and on other planets.

We wish at this time to speak only of the effect that so many incarnations as a human being, bound up in the bonds of karma, have had upon your spirit, and how, enduring them all, your spirit continually longs for the joy and freedom it once knew.

The dynamics of your relationships with other people affect and in many ways reflect the state of the planet, as well as your own health and that of others. Even other planets are affected indirectly, because the waves of vibration from thought and action pass into the universe.

Alignment at St. Pierre-Quiberon

Like electromagnetic fields, these waves are not limited in space; everything, from the subatomic to the cosmic, is connected with everything else in a web of many invisible fields of energy.

Previous life relationships have a direct effect in that numerous souls have become trapped between the etheric and physical planes, prevented from moving on because of human negligence and emotional karma. This clogging of the atmosphere has in turn obstructed other souls from coming in to gain experience of life on Earth. Moreover, the same souls repeatedly return, so there are fewer opportunities for others who have never incarnated on Earth to do so.

Your own family situation is directly linked to your ancestral karma, and certain situations have been attracted to you by the earthly laws of cause and effect. Throughout numerous incarnations, most of you have had many families and relationships, some pleasant, some difficult, in which you have played different roles, all experiences that accumulate to influence your present life. In general we can say that your various lives tend to occur within the same group of other incarnated souls, who return incessantly in order to be together and resolve their past difficulties.

Souls experience both male and female embodiments. At various times you have been a brother, sister, mother, or father, as well as wife, husband, son, or daughter. You may have been a priest or nun, a beggar or slave, a soldier, perhaps a trader or peasant farmer. You have been both rich and poor, experiencing abundance and the lack of it. You may, for example, have made a vow of poverty as a monk in one incarnation which is still resonating within your present life, and you wonder why you never have enough for your needs. Alternatively, you may have made a vow of chastity, and so you always feel guilty about sexual relationships. Old attitudes such as these persist because they are in your subconscious, but they can be reversed by awareness and your own conscious intention.

In each lifetime, therefore, there are choices to be made which will affect your destiny. On each occasion the same souls have come together, although not necessarily in the same family. Sometimes they choose a different family so that new relationships can be formed and others be resolved, and they may reunite with their soul family at a later stage. You resemble a troupe of actors, always in rehearsal of the different parts. As you become fully incarnate, aware and responsible, you will no longer be rehearsing, but living out your life on the world's stage.

Many people become stuck in the same role, unable to move out of it even though the external circumstances of a life may not be appropriate for its continuation. The identification with that role and its hidden memories may overwhelm them. It is as though they carry the same set of clothes around with them life after life, until the realization dawns that another wardrobe, other opportunities, are open to them. Too many lifetimes that were set, for example, in a background of religious hierarchy, as master or as servant, have created subconscious patterns of behavior that affect your present attitudes.

It is important to look below the surface of your relationships to try to see clearly the motivation and dynamics involved in each situation, changing what you can when necessary and recognizing what may be a karmic recurrence in the evolutionary journey of your soul. You see, there can be no evolution, no inner peace, until this cycle of recurring patterns is broken, and the soul is able to free itself from the restrictions of its past history.

As human soul families evolve in a more enlightened way, they will be stepping over the old limitations and may free themselves from the bondage and seeming security of their earthly family unit. Once the soul recognizes that the family relationship has become restrictive to its further development, it will be impelled to seek change. We do not say that this is always the case; but if it is, you will be feeling that you are out of place within your own family, that you are expected to continue playing a role that you have grown out of. Your soul will no longer see the promise of fulfillment in continuing to play a role that serves no creative purpose. To continue acting that part will restrict not only your own development but also that of other family members. By seeking your own freedom, you give others a chance to find their own.

There is a challenge for you all in finding your soul family group; for some this is happening now, because many have released themselves from the old harness of karma and rediscovered a certain liberty of spirit. Some members of earthly families are discovering that they are already part of the same soul group, so there is much warmth and joy in the relationships between them. Many others have yet to recognize their karmic situations, and so have yet to break free and find kinship within their soul group. These dispersed but effective regroupings are the first steps toward a more widespread and meaningful reunification of humankind.

Some of the Native Americans had an understanding of the workings of karma. Knowing they would return to live in another body after the death of the present one, they acted out each lifetime with a certain level of awareness and foreknowledge. If one caused harm to another, the transgressor would not be rejected. It was understood that any difficult situation could give rise to karmic retribution, and wisely they did their best to effect healing within the current lifetime. This may not always have been successful, but the positive intention was there.

In your lives today we observe that you reject anything that displeases you, attempting to rid yourselves of people or situations that you consider unpleasant or ugly. But in doing this you simply become more entangled. You have not accepted that the karmic powers of creation—both dark and light—are at work in every situation, in a totality which your restricted attitudes do not allow you to perceive. Whatever you reject out of fear or hatred attaches itself to you like ivy growing around a tree; you can only free yourself from such issues through acceptance. You will find that simply by changing your attitude toward a situation, the situation itself changes. Your consciousness of a new perspective and your introduction of more light can actually change circumstances for the better.

Many, many incarnations have been lived through, each one offering you opportunities to find and follow your destiny. There has been so much unfinished business, as the events of one lifetime ricochet into the next, pinning souls to the Earth's plane, that they must return again and again to resolve the problems they have created for themselves.

The law of karma evolved to allow a healing process to take place. This was appropriate and necessary, since it allowed for another run-through of whatever issues had not been resolved. But the saboteur within you, the shadow of the dark, has ensured forgetfulness from one incarnation to the next. Karma, as you understand it, is not a cosmic law; it is an earthly pattern. You were never intended to become so entrapped by the negative emotions that bind your spirit. Guilt, blame, and remorse create attachments which remain to torment you even when the events are long forgotten by your conscious mind. Thus each return is often no more than a repeat of the previous life, and each time more karma is incurred. This has tied the spirit to the Earth for longer than was intended and resulted in more entanglements in each new lifetime, with very little learned. But now there is no longer time for all this rep-etition; karma has become more or less instantaneous. The time frame you have previously perceived is changing.

All of you have an innate capacity to love, a potential to forgive yourself and others that can release you from the seemingly endless drama. Whereas in times past there was always the need for a compen-satory process to balance each original act, now you have the possibil-ity of freeing yourselves from the grip of past circumstances by living totally in the present and acting always with compassion, love, and discernment.

Although the people of Egypt learned much from the Atlanteans who settled among them, this was later distorted and lost. They recognized the need of the spirit, after bodily death, to return to its home in the skies, but their customary process of mummification to preserve the body made the return incomplete. Because the body was not returned to the elements—omitting an important stage in the cycle of earthly life— the evolutionary process was halted. In the incarnations which followed, those whose bodies had been preserved often had to experience life with a sickness such as leprosy in order to complete the cycle in a sort of living death. This is an example of what happens when cosmic law is forgotten and humans invent their own. It is cosmic law that the vehicle of life be returned to the elements of which it is made. If this does not happen, it simply creates a karmic debt to the universe. Since, in the early days, those whose bodies were mummified—the pharaohs, the nobles, and the priests—were of the ruling class, they were condemned to live out a following incarnation in humble and unpleasant circumstances. The purpose of the process was to avoid reincarnation, as it was assumed that the initiates of the secret mysteries had evolved sufficiently to free their spirits for immortality. The Egyptians were concerned to provide all that was needed for the afterlife, believing that what was provided physically, including the body, would also be there at the etheric level.

The Christian Church has long denied the fact of reincarnation, not because it is untrue, but because it requires an acceptance of cosmic law that would weaken its earthly authority and open the way to direct spiritual awareness.

An understanding of karma and the prospect of reincarnation opens the way to greater individual power and responsibility, along with the freedom to make life's choices with greater clarity. Many people unfortunately give away their power, either in obedience to old religious precepts by surrendering to an organization that has become rich and powerful at their expense, or in heedless pursuit of the conventional goals of an acquisitive society. It is essential that you see this clearly and become responsible for yourselves as individuals. Until you do, you cannot assume responsibility for the planet; and this, as you are becoming aware, is vital for us all.

When you take full authority over yourself you are released from karma. You let go of blame, whether of self or of others, freeing yourself to follow your true destiny. By accepting personal responsibility in any predicament, you are enabled to see that nobody acts against you or does you harm without the implicit permission of your own soul. You are no longer in the position of blaming someone else. You have to look at why you, yourself, attract the circumstances that require you to experience suffering in the form of humiliation, rejection, loss, or hardship, and then see what opportunities there are for you to turn the situation around. You chose to be born into a certain family situation and location that would present you with the appropriate circumstances to experience whatever was needed for your development. Other people are simply acting out their own drama of unfoldment, alongside and interacting with yours, "pressing your buttons" if you like. But the element of choice is always present, even if it is not easy to recognize.

If you can be thankful to circumstances for offering you a lesson, teaching what you need to know, perhaps liberating you from illusions which have caused you pain and suffering, then you are no longer a victim. You are recovering your own self-possession, a state in which you can move through life with Grace and restore your connection with the divine.

For many of you it is as though you pass through each life half-conscious, sleepwalking around the mind of the establishment, accepting without question its authority over your own. Such an attitude has served as a playpen for confining the human soul, a restriction in which family histories have been acted out. Now that you are growing up, you can see that the bars you thought were there to protect you have become a prison—as indeed almost all human authority, when lacking in divine wisdom, has always been.

Many of your long-accepted ideas are falsehoods of human invention. Even if not designed for the purpose, they have limited the spread of true human comprehension. The dualistic concept of heaven and hell, for example, is a simplistic illusion by which you have actually created your own heavens and hells here on Earth, in the neat compartments of good and evil, the superficial judgments of right and wrong, the handing out of punishment or reward. The rules of society fragment and compartmentalize; they do not, cannot, encompass the whole.

If those who compiled the Christian Bible had understood the message of Jesus and had been permitted to tell the complete story with freedom and clarity, it would not now be so necessary to impart this message. The adherents of other world religions have also fallen into intolerance and fanaticism, for they too have been misled by ignorance and the deliberate misinterpretation of their holy books. Organized religion has become political, more concerned with power than spiritual inspiration. The dark has been in control for so long. Now is the time for Love to return and bring back the power of the light.

Your soul cannot return to the Creator in a wounded condition. If you are damaged in spirit, you will return to the scene where your wounds were received or to the people who inflicted them, remembering that they also are wounded. Only when you extract yourself from these karmic bonds by healing your own wounds, learning from both past and present, making different choices with healthier outcomes, can you return whole in spirit to the Creator, with the freedom to continue your soul's journey in other, higher spheres.

Sometimes this healing can be effected in spirit, in the consciousness which continues after death of the physical body, by those souls who are committed to helping others to evolve out of past traumas. When this process is completed, a choice can be made as to whether to return to Earth. The decision may be not to return, but to give service in spirit; when the decision is to return in body, the clear intention of a healed soul will be not to create more darkness but to bring in clarity and Love. With that choice, you will be a torchbearer for the truth.

Every human being is a divine spark, a chip off the old block, as you might say. You are all essence of the Creator. The realization of this will give you the strength to summon those inner resources and to connect with the help that we can lovingly give you, which is the reason for our existence.

When you were innocent and uncommitted, you were given a choice of whether to work with the forces of light or those of darkness. You have found difficulty in distinguishing between them, sometimes allowing the forces of darkness to work through you while believing them to be of the light. It has been difficult to transcend the cruelty and suffering of the world which many have experienced as the human lot, leading to doubt as to the very existence of a Creator. How could God allow such things to happen? The answer is simple. God is Love, and loving is allowing; allowing you to learn discernment through the exercise of your own choice. It is humans themselves who make such things happen by choosing to do them, by their lack of compassion. There can be divine intervention only when the power of prayer and Love around a situation outweighs the darkness and ignorance and allows in the higher vibrations. We, all of us in the cosmos, are waiting for human beings to wake up to the power of Love.

Terrible things—we see that as meaning actions without love for one another or for the Earth—have been done through fear. The world has seen an almost endless recycling of the same souls, struggling to learn to work with the forces of the material world, endeavoring to transform their shadows into light. Souls deriving from one planet have sometimes been born to parents of quite another origin, if this served to correct some previous conflict or disharmony or simply to provide a different environment for growth. Parents have learned to feel love for children who, in another lifetime, may well have been their enemies and caused great anguish. When tribes and nations have fought and killed each other in war, their souls have sometimes come back to reincarnate in the opposing camp in order to understand their enemies' perspective, and bring about understanding between the two sides. In this manner one who was a crusader may well have an incarnation as a Muslim, and in America many of the white settlers have returned to a life among the Indian tribes they once decimated.

Souls never die, but they can suffer. Looking at you now, we see that there is plenty of suffering and many spurious and misleading values. Your lack of sufficient awareness to call spirit into matter, a failure that further darkens the human psyche, destroys the ability to enjoy daily life in a magical way. It leaves you without a higher purpose, at a less-than-human level where you easily surrender to emotions, to false goals and the impositions of others.

As you move toward a future that will connect you with the higher levels of vibratory life, we ask you to open yourself to the presence of miracles. Regain your vision, the clear insight that you had before your birth. Each of you carries an etheric blueprint that shows the purpose of your life and the earthly path you are intended to follow. When your present incarnation was planned, a particular place on the planet and a particular group of people drew your soul to them with a magnetic attraction, because of past links and unfinished business from previous incarnations. Yet it is all one life, with a different vehicle for

Le Cosquer Dolmen

each rebirth and incarnation. Each is a different aspect of that one life, flowing perpetually toward the Creator.

Every return is an effort to correct the balance, to get back on course and move to a deeper awareness of your relationship with the planet, and to gain understanding of the Earth's relationship with creation as a whole.

Each of you, then, is given a direction to follow when you incarnate on this Earth. Before your spirit became enmeshed in matter, you knew in your inner being what it was you had returned for, and what issues needed to be addressed. As infants you were still in touch with your vision. For most of you this has slowly faded as you accommodated to the world and tried to match the expectations of those around you, especially those of adults who had by then lost their own inner purpose and succumbed to society's conventions. Thus your own private vision becomes just a fantasy or daydream, impossible to realize in a milieu so circumscribed by adult rules.

The daydreaming of children, for which they are so often punished, is a way of keeping contact with other worlds, of keeping in touch with the instincts of the right brain. Young children are close to the realms of spirit and sometimes remain aware of their own spirit guides for many years. Spirit guides are recognized by Eastern cultures, but usually dismissed by peoples of the "developed" West, who are either too busy or too cynically unreflective to sense what is around them in the unseen world. Innocence, inner sense, and mystery have been lost to busy-ness; but daydreaming is important, as it may lead to inspiration, the revelation of hidden truth that can never be found by the logical mind. Some of your scientists have discovered this in reaching the solution to an intractable problem, intuitively and unexpectedly. And for people such as the aboriginal Australians, the "dreamtime" is still an accessible route to another face of reality that exists beside and is interwoven with daily life. As such, it has long been respected by them as embracing the spirits of the ancestors, the souls of the animal kingdom, and the elemental beings of nature.

You have been diverted from your true destiny in order to fit the requirements of human society at the expense of the individual spirit. You have become burdened by the weight of ancestral and personal unresolved problems. The upside is that there is much scope for spiritual growth, which we assure you will take place alongside the resolution of those other difficulties.

One of your Bible teachings tells you that it takes several generations to clear the legacy of an inherited karma. This has been true in the past but will not be the case in the future, since everything that remains unresolved is now coming to the surface, unavoidably and finally to be dealt with in the present.

All of you have ancestors within your own family tree who at this present time need your help to turn to the light. They have not been able to help themselves and need your recognition of their condition before they can be released. Some of them want simply to say that they love you before they go forward. Others, however, because of their emotional entanglement with past physical circumstances, or due to the manner of their dying, are unable to experience a joyous release. You can change this in a simple ceremony, by lighting a candle of remembrance for them, by feeling love in your heart for them, and at the same time by asking for the presence of the Archangels to take them to the light. If you are aware of such trapped souls, you can in that way release them and restore healing energy to the family.

Remember that this small ceremony may also need to include the unborn, the miscarriages and terminated pregnancies that so many women experience. All have souls which need to be acknowledged and to have experience of human love before they move back into the light, ready for birth on another occasion. We remind you here that there need be no guilt or blame around such situations; there is always the freedom to choose, and many of these souls have had no intention of incarnating. They only wish to make contact, perhaps with those they have already known and loved; or even to bring a little disruptive energy into a life that needs to take a new direction. But in all these cases a naming, a recognition, and yes, a celebration of release is as vital for that soul's journey onward as it is for those remaining in the physical world. However, there are times when to deny the possibility of a new life is to oppose the life flow and all the opportunities offered. The denial then will have negative repercussions—it is never the end of the story.

If a soul is not at peace from past events, there may be unrest within the family, even mental instability, as an unquiet spirit will always cry out for help by putting something out of balance, wanting to make others feel its distress. When mental illness is not a soul's choice to experience but results from interference of that sort, it usually signifies an unquiet ancestor. Your own bonding with your soul purpose or your life's progress may then be delayed and things may appear to go awry. Ancestral energy of that type needs to be released by your prayers of love, when a vast amount of energy can be directed toward what is beneficial for your life, bringing help to you just as you have given help.

We see to it that there are always opportunities for you to find your rightful direction, and it is for every one of you to recognize the signposts along the way. Which points to an opportunity and which to a diversion? You are all learning discernment. It is your responsibility to listen to the inner promptings, to trust your own intuition, which will help you to develop a sense of purpose and provide the guidance you need to pass through this incarnation and on to the next, motivated only by the Love of the Creator.

Alignment at Le Petit Ménec

CHAPTER 13

A Glimpse of the Future

Many waters cannot quench love, neither can the floods drown it.

—The Song of Solomon

Karma, as humans have been experiencing it, is coming to an end in this lifetime. Previously there was time to reincarnate into another body, another life, in order to deal with unresolved issues from a previous lifetime. There is no longer room for this as certain time cycles are coming to a close with the move into the Aquarian age and new ones are beginning. There are cosmic changes taking place, and the swinging pendulum is about to pause before it goes the other way. Most human karma will be resolved in the present lifetime, sometimes instantaneously with scarcely a gap between action and reaction. Often a person will have two seemingly incompatible lifestyles running alongside each other, fitting two lifetimes' experiences into one.

There is a saying, "When my ship comes in," referring to a time when a person's fortune was aboard ship in goods. Well, all your ships will be coming in and the harbor will seem very crowded. Some of the boats will be full of treasure, some will bring other kinds of surprises. Everything you have deserved for your highest good but have not yet received will come to you. What has not been resolved within this time scale will have to be worked on in other dimensions when the spirit has left the body, and that will create a lot more work for the hosts of angels.

Reincarnation is coming to an end also. Very few humans will be allowed to return, and for most, this is their last incarnation. That is why at times there seem to be so many obstacles and so many opportunities all in the same place! Fewer people will be on the planet in the times to come and those few will not have karma to resolve. Instead, theirs will be the task of creating the Golden City, the New Jerusalem. Their work will be set upon what is achieved now in terms of resolving all karma in a positive manner. These people will come from other planets and other galaxies who have not previously had an opportunity to incarnate upon the Earth, and there will also be those who have been the dolphins. We can say, too, that some of the Archangels will incarnate on Earth; it will be as it was in the beginning, but with greater spiritual strength on Earth. Human beings in general have not reached a high enough level of consciousness within the time we had hoped. There will be a grinding to a halt, and at the same time there will be a new beginning for planet Earth. Present human consciousness will continue to evolve elsewhere.

268

You can expect many changes as you learn to be more constructive and responsible in your attitudes, not only toward yourselves and one another, but toward planet Earth and the cosmos as a whole.

The times to come will see children born who are free from karma, who do not bring with them personal issues from the past to resolve. These children will be fully incarnate, filled with a positive life force and a strong sense of inner direction. They will be directly linked in their intuitive wisdom to the creative forces. In them, the left and right hemispheres of the brain will be in perfect balance. Their loving and harmonious personalities will express themselves by making your planet into a sacred place, re-creating it as the Garden it is intended to be.

Perception for so many people has been, and is still, clouded by the negative attitudes so common on Earth. Negative thoughts, whether personified or acted out, prevent you from stepping fully into life with the love which is so beautifully celebrated in the Song of Solomon. They cause the very air you breathe to carry fear, they are the origin of so much pain, setting false goals for individuals and imposing distorted values upon society. These sad feelings of restriction and helplessness arise from the historic perversion of every spiritual truth that has been given to you and from the human inability to reach back to the original wisdom of the masters. Nevertheless, the truth is in safekeeping for you. The deep sense of oppression which has resulted from its loss is beginning to lift as more of you are connecting with your own intuitive integrity and your own life guidance.

The way forward is to surrender only to what is highest in you. There will be no room for negative emotions to dominate. You will learn to use your thoughts wisely, rather than being used by them. The conscious mind is awakening from a deep sleep of thousands of years. Despite—and perhaps because of—the inhumanity and scale of the savage events of the century just past, many human beings are rousing themselves, waking up with a new love in their hearts which desires to end the suffering. The changes that lie ahead are concerned with living in full consciousness, in the wisdom of your own hearts. We tell you plainly that this has never happened before.

Love is an unlimited energy that you have seldom tapped into. It is the most dynamic energy that exists. The purity of Love, uncontaminated by any desire for domination, can lighten any situation and bring clarity to all areas of darkness in the world. Accept the difference of others, love the beauty and variety of that difference instead of finding it threatening, allow it to enhance the whole and celebrate it with joy.

Many still resist love, feeling that they do not deserve it or cannot trust it, and keeping it at arm's length. They feel unable to match up to it, or perhaps are afraid of losing it if it is acknowledged. But we tell you your hearts will be opened and you will feel love.

Love is the guardian of the truth, Love sustains, Love exalts and enriches; the Love of the Creator is the rightful inheritance of every human being.

The objective of your present incarnation is the healing of karmic wounds and the transformation of old negative emotions—those which went against the natural flow because they excluded Love—into true feeling. Love will guide you through the shadows into acceptance and joy. Human beings need to become whole-hearted. When your heart is whole it is big enough to love the world, even to lighten the universe. Fear, and the hatred it produces, can never lead you to the truth. Rather, it simply serves to hide the light of the Creator from you. Only when you love life will you be free to consciously pursue your destiny wherever it may lead, and to work positively with the flow of life upon your planet.

As you are realizing, the Earth is a living being that inhales, exhales, and continues to evolve as part of a pulsating, ever-expanding universe. Deep within its etheric structure is a memory of the divine plan, a blueprint of the original intention. We have described some of the inputs of our Archangelic energy with which your planet has to work; when they are disrupted by human ignorance and carelessness, the Earth is aware of the disturbance. Just like the human body in sickness, it has an innate power to return to a condition of healthy balance. In the course of the body's recovery there is often a fever and much moaning and groaning. If something has entered the body that disagrees with the system, it has to pass through it to be eliminated, and every part and organ is aware of the process. This is what can be predicted for planet Earth. Although it is easier to clear the pollution from the planet than it is to clear it from the minds of human beings, the return to order will be accompanied by much rearrangement and unexpected change; there will be discomfort in this for many of you.

There are, therefore, events to come for which humankind needs to be prepared. There will be periods of both inner and outer turmoil, especially for those whose spirits have not yet reached toward the light for guidance. There will be times of choice and challenge which may create what you would call breakdowns in people's lives, certainly the breakdown of old attitudes and systems of belief. It will be an opportunity for you all either to redirect yourselves to the truth, or to stay within the old familiar framework and crumble with it; for crumble away it must, since it is not supported by any spiritual truth.

The fulfillment of its destiny is essential for the evolution of every soul, and evolution takes place through an enlargement of the state of consciousness. The destiny of each of you is therefore to evolve consciously, through the body in life and out of it at death, in order to rejoin that greater part of your soul of which this present incarnation is only a fragment. Every previous incarnation has been such a fragment of the whole; your soul has never been totally present here on Earth. With every new insight gained on an emotional, mental, or spiritual level, there is a corresponding change or release on a physical and cellular level. This can bring pain as the body adapts to the release of tension and the expansion brings you into new patterns of energy. This is what is meant by evolving through the body.

Each incarnation has focused on whatever part of the jigsaw is needed to complete the ultimate picture. As this becomes recognizable, the conscious mind awakens and it becomes possible to be totally present, fully incarnate. When there is no more karma to resolve, there will no longer be a necessity to return to Earth, except for those who choose to commit themselves to the building of the New Jerusalem. But evolution is not just about resolving karma; it is also about the combining of matter with spirit. Without the guiding light of spiritual nourishment, you are in danger of remaining entrenched in your material world, hypnotized by its technological advances.

There is a fundamental order in the cosmos, of which you form an important part, which cannot be tampered with—not without risking a devastating outcome. Whatever has been damaged on one level will inevitably work to repair itself on another. On the planetary scale this will mean movements of the earth, air, and water. On a personal and parallel level, upheavals in human relationships are bound to occur when you have gone against the grain for so long, when you still have karma to resolve or a destiny to follow in some other place. You may see that this has begun to happen in the loosening and fragmentation of your society and your families that began after the First World War.

Regaining trust in yourself and learning to be yourself are both of the utmost importance. If you do not trust yourself through a lack of connection with your highest self, you surrender control to others who will make decisions for you. How can you trust those who are merely practiced in leadership and desirous of governance when they are not in touch with their inner guidance? This situation effectively puts you on hold, as it were, and while it may be comfortable for a time, it achieves nothing. It is the blind leading the blind.

To take off the dark glasses and see more clearly your own motivation and that of others, and so act more wisely and appropriately, there must always be a space for inner silence, the dreamtime, the quiet attunement to nature and the other realms of being. In this inner communion you can refuel yourself, drawing in the spiritual sustenance that in full consciousness you cannot live without. In that way you can acknowledge and respond to the energies at work in your life with a positive rather than a negative strength. Learn to listen; it is vital, and yet so many of you have lost the art of inner listening.

Past patterns of dominance and subservience have persuaded you to relinquish your power to those with a stronger will, and this makes you extremely vulnerable to anyone with a powerful charisma but no integrity. Such a person will be appearing on the world scene and will fully test your ability to be discerning. As a charismatic leader, a friend to all, saying what many wounded hearts wish to hear, this impressive personality will have great influence for a time, but eventually will prove false. We warn you to be on your guard; remember that the heart, which is in tune with the Christ consciousness, will remain in the light and be unaffected. There may be some of the Jewish faith who consider this to be the promised messiah, but it will be an illusion.

In past incarnations, danger has often arisen from speaking your own truth, which has led to persecution and suffering. This time the danger lies in failing to speak your own truth, and in consequence being unable to live it. The desire to act a part—any reluctance to be yourself—has to be overcome. Since this charismatic being will seem to shine in the eyes of many, there will be a tendency for individuality to be lost as many are caught up in the mass vision of a false utopia. This powerful leader, exerting influence over large areas of Europe and North America, will be using other people's psychic energy to support personal ambition. There may be a general belief that this is the Savior whom many are expecting, since people still look outside themselves for leadership. Some will think it is the second coming of Christ. They do not realize that the true second coming will occur within the human heart and the conscious mind at the birthing of a new era. Those who are seduced by the charisma of this person will appear to others as though they are blindfolded, unable to see the truth.

There will be a certain parting of the ways and it will be a time of testing for all of you, but since learning discernment is part of the soul's task, it will be an interesting time also. From the time of the emergence of this false prophet there will be a very short period—possibly no more than a few years—before the final dissolution of your religious and political institutions in their present form. This will be a time of great confusion as the light and the dark are weighed against each other. There will be a cleansing in preparation for a vision of the future in which spiritual truth is honored once more; but you will be living very much in the moment, with little opportunity to think about or plan for it. As you become free from karmic pressures, truth will be expressed spontaneously as Love and integrity (not regarded as now, as something that has to be questioned, pondered, or legislated). It will be instantly recognizable because a state of Grace will be with you. You will become, as the Master Jesus said, innocent as little children, free from negative influence. Those who still retain unworthy attitudes will remain under the sway of their lower emotions and will have no access to wisdom, for wisdom is attended by Grace; but they will no longer be in the majority. The false messiah will depart, and there will be a further weakening of the various organizations that shape and limit your present social structures before the human race can enter upon the long-predicted era of peace.

We must tell you that there is likely to be further turmoil, this time caused by the possibility of collision with an asteroid. The point of impact will be in that part of the planet where the final stages of the battle between the light and dark forces are to be enacted, the vortex area in which so much activity and conflict have occurred since the Fall. There are echoes of past conflicts elsewhere, but it is in the Middle East that they are strongest. If the peoples of those lands, the Arabs and the Israelis, can finally recognize with joy that they are of one soul family, realize that forgiveness and acceptance are a necessary part of their evolutionary growth, and learn to live with each other's positive aspects instead of the traditional hostility, there will be a wonderful sharing of wisdom that can affect the vibrations of the whole planet. In fact, the joy that would be released through neighborly acceptance in such troubled parts of the world would create enough positive energy to divert the asteroid.

We have spoken about restoration, the revival of spiritual values, and how the impact of negative events can be lessened by a more widespread human understanding of the difference between spiritual truth and man-made law. Even as an individual, the way in which each of you lives your life has always made a difference to the whole and it will continue to do so. Nevertheless, the asteroid danger threatens because the power of attraction is already present; but there are a sufficient number of years in Earth time before that event can occur. There is time to become more positive and more whole-hearted. There is time to change the attitudes and priorities with which you work on Earth, to abandon the greed of those who have plenty and still want more, and the resentment of those who have not. Actions which enhance the quality of life without distorting or opposing its natural rhythms are essential. This is a time for deeds, not words. To focus anxiously on the asteroid itself will not be beneficial, as it will only divert your mind from positive action.

This adoption of a more positive lifestyle by a large number of people can create a positive field of energy that will be powerful enough to prevent, and can certainly minimize, the event we speak of. When hope in the heart is realized through a strong commitment to Love, all things are possible. For each of you, this is your personal and social obligation at this time. If you cannot accept this, nor take personal responsibility for aligning your own will to that of the Creator, then we tell you that the planet will take charge. There will be another pause in the development of the human soul, a further delay in returning to the Creator. Take but a single step in the right direction and we shall be with you.

Many of you give up too easily at the first difficulty, not understanding that you are affected by the fluctuating wave patterns of energy that are always at work on the planet, causing the ups and downs that are part of the flow of life. Accept the rhythm of change, learn to ride the wave and aim for the middle way of balance.

Alignment at Kerlescan

The necessary changes in the human condition and general level of consciousness will take place through an increase of energy reaching the chakras of the body, a process that has already begun. Likewise, changes have also begun in the Earth's vibratory fields through a strengthening of the solar and Jupiter forces which are received and held at the sacred sites. The more human love is expressed through compassion, the more the Earth will respond positively, and the more it will be felt beyond the Earth, reducing the threat from the asteroid belt and creating more harmonious conditions within the atmosphere.

We wish now to speak of certain other forms of disturbance which are likely to occur within human beings, who will need appropriate attention and loving care. There are many sensitive people who have never experienced true spiritual nourishment and often these people become confused and saddened. Life makes no sense to them and they find it difficult to cope with. Their potential goes unrecognized, perhaps because they have never had a chance to blossom in a loving environment or within your educational system. This can cause a withdrawal and reactions of resentment or hatred, and hatred is the reverse side of love.

As long as children continue to be brought up in a judgmental society there will be those who are not accepted. In later life the pain of separation from Love and a lack of self-esteem causes such people to go around with a psychic sign over their heads that says SPACE TO LET. At a certain level of the unconscious mind they are offering vacant possession, and the sign can be read on the astral level where there are plenty of spirits waiting for such an opportunity. An exchange can take place, and you may have witnessed such an event; the overuse of drugs can precipitate it. It only can happen if permission is given, unconsciously at the soul level, when something can be learned from the experience.

When such a spirit enters a person's mind, a different personality will emerge and the obvious change is likely to alarm family and friends.

All spirits who take over in this way have unfinished business related to the progress of their own ego; they are tricksters, using flattery and promises to gain "possession." As in the story of Faust, the owner of the body is promised the reward of success but is then left helpless, suspended by a thread, while the usurper makes use of the available body. In effect, two spirits compete for the same mind, and the owner is unable to return without summoning enormous willpower—which is what was lacking in the first place. If what is happening is recognized, a healing exorcism can be carried out, in a compassionate way, which will release the usurper into the light and on to a higher level of vibration. This allows the owner back in to take up a more permanent residence, but it is possible only if he or she is willing to return and feels enough support from those around to do so. If the situation is not dealt with in a careful and healing manner, however, the struggle may be continued in one of your institutions for mental health, with damage to both spirits from the use of symptom-controlling drugs. In the past such intrusions were regarded as possession by the devil, but to be more accurate, these are unenlightened spirits from the astral plane who need help; spirits from the light do not interfere in this way.

We have been concerned with telling you about your origins, the past and present distortions of the truth, and the responsibility each of you bears for yourself and for the way in which you live upon the Earth. Knowing your true birthright, the inheritance of Love, you have the ability to heal yourselves and one another. Our influence, borne on the networks of solar and planetary energy, is constantly around you, and our help will always be given to those who ask. We can say with certainty that all human energy will eventually come to a point of balance and harmony, however difficult, painful, or lengthy the process may seem.

You are not humans on a spiritual journey, you are spirit on a human journey, and as such you need spiritual as well as physical sustenance. Air, water, and food provide the fuel for your body, but the magic that makes life itself has its origin in spirit.

To assist these journeys, we have programmed other stones with further information for those who live in different parts of the world; those stones, too, will be found in time and the messages decoded. We do not say that they are the same, for they will relate more specifically to the future and to the areas in which they are located. There are encoded stones in the country now called Poland, some near the Great Wall of China, and others waiting to be found at the appropriate time in northern Canada.

For the future of humankind, spiritual nourishment will be the food of life; with it you will become conscious co-creators, using the power of thought rather than being its servant. Instead of creating your reality subconsciously through inherited fear and dark thoughts, you will begin to create it consciously from the soul, bringing the purity of light through your chakras into the love of your heart. The development of humanity will take place in an acknowledged connection with the mind of the Universe, healing the minds of humans in the experience of unity instead of separation.

281

The journey through physical life will teach you to bless life and to be blessed by it, and lead you to fulfillment.

Love is the energy that created the Universe. Loving is living in harmony; we are Love and so can you be. All of us are one in the Love of the Creator, which we offer and you can manifest.

Our blessings be upon you all.

Glossary

Alignment A prehistoric row of standing stones set up for ritual purposes, many in multiple rows or avenues. The alignments are especially concentrated near the small town of Carnac in Brittany, France, where the longest is called Le Ménec.

Brittany, or *La Bretagne* The old department of France facing the Atlantic Ocean. Long independent, it has its own language, *Breton,* which is closely allied to Welsh and Cornish. There were strong trading and cultural links with Britain in Neolithic and Bronze Age times. Like its alternative, Little Britain in the Arthurian legends, the name is a reflection of early British immigration.

Cairn A heap of stones, usually covering a prehistoric tomb, found in Ireland, Spain, France, and many other countries of the world. Carnac is "the village by the cairn" known as Tumulus St. Michel (see the final photograph in this book).

Chakra Sanskrit for wheel or circle, describing one of a number of unseen, non-corporeal links in the body that receive and transform for its use, subtle external energy fields. The chakras are usually perceived as dynamic spirals of energy.

Chambered mound A man-made mound of earth containing a stone-built chamber to hold the bones of the dead. Some of the mounds around Carnac are exceptionally large.

Cromlech A circular or curved arrangement of closely set standing stones in Brittany, often placed at the end of an *alignment* for use in ceremonial assemblies. It is a Welsh word, confusingly used in Britain for a *dolmen.*

Crop circles Mysterious patterns of unknown origin, often incorporating circular forms, impressed into standing summer crops in England and less commonly in many other countries. They are characterized by the regular swirl of the crop stems, which are laid flat on the ground without any break in the stems. Many have been photographed from the air over a number of years, and often they refer to our planetary system; others appear to be a sort of cosmic joke. They are located on solar or Jupiter energy lines. Around Avebury and Stonehenge in summer 1988, fifty-one crop circles appeared, each different.

Dolmen The Breton word, meaning table-stones, for a large, flat-topped stone chamber or tomb structure, now usually exposed but once within a mound or *cairn.*

Dowsing Traditionally the use of a Y-shaped hazel twig to locate water underground, extended now to the use of handheld rods or a pendulum for other purposes such as the detection of energy fields around the earth (for example, the so-called leylines), or around a person (that is, their aura or chakras). Dowsing may also be used to locate unseen or lost objects (as on a map, or below ground, such as archaeological remains or service pipes) and for diagnostic and healing purposes.

Enclosure A stone or earthen surround to an area of ground for ritual use.

Karma Sanskrit for action, meaning the active force of creation in a unified universe. The word is found in traditional Indian writings. The present meaning of an endless chain of cause and effect by which the actions of one human life lead to reactions in the next is derived from Buddhist beliefs.

Leyline The common, but confusing, term for a line or band of solar energy, not visible but detectable by dowsing. Leylines link sacred sites all over the world in what the observer sees as straight alignments. In fact, since they extend over long distances they follow the curvature of the Earth, and some form great circles around the globe. Many significant places and ancient structures are located on them; medicine wheels and mounds in North America; temples in India, Egypt, China, Japan, and South America; burial mounds and standing stones in Europe and elsewhere. Many of the latter were replaced or reused (sometimes with the intention of neutralizing them), by Christian churches or Muslim mosques in medieval times. A more accurate term would be *solar line.*

Megalith A great stone erected by prehistoric people, singly or in groups, such as the British stone circles or the Brittany *alignments*.

Menhir The Breton term, meaning long stone, for an upright, isolated *megalith*.

Neolithic An invented word for the late Stone Age of prehistory, ending in Europe about four thousand years ago, when bronze tools began to supersede those made from stone.

Tumulus The Latin word for a burial mound.

Tumulus St. Michel in Carnac

ABOUT THE AUTHORS

NATASHA HOFFMAN earned a degree in Fine Art and for twenty years taught Art and Design at Hastings College of Art. Seeking to work with others in a more personal way, Hoffman studied kinesiology and left teaching to pursue individual healings through kinesiology and her intuition. Aware of a heightened intuitive ability at an early age, Hoffman's skill was honed over time and brought her to the stones at Carnac. In addition to her intuitive and healing work, she is a practicing artist who continues to exhibit her work.

HAMILTON HILL was senior partner of a London surveying firm after graduating from Oxford University with an M.A. in History. Hill left urban life to operate a 200-acre farm in Sussex for several years. At present, he designs private gardens and is an active member of the British Society of Dowsers.

Hoffman and Hill divide their time between their home in Devon, England, and a house they are restoring in France.